The Best of
CAJUN & CREOLE COOKING

The Best of
CAJUN & CREOLE COOKING

Alex Barker

Gramercy Books
New York

This 2003 edition is published by
Gramercy Books, an imprint of
Random House Value Publishing, a
division of Random House, Inc.,
New York.

Gramercy is a registered trademark and
the colophon is a trademark of
Random House, Inc.

Random House
New York•Toronto•London•Sydney•
Auckland
www.randomhouse.com

Printed and bound in Italy

All photography supplied by
Food Features

A catalog record for this title is
available from the Library of Congress

ISBN 0-517-21842-9

10 9 8 7 6 5 4 3 2 1

CONTENTS

APPETIZERS

CALLALOO (below)

Callaloo is a thick spicy soup made with dasheen (taro) leaves, which are available from Caribbean or other specialty stores. If you can't find them, use fresh spinach instead.

Serves 6

INGREDIENTS:
12 oz dasheen leaves or 1 lb fresh young spinach
1 tbsp butter
1 tbsp vegetable oil
1 onion, finely chopped
2 cloves of garlic, crushed
4 oz okra, trimmed and sliced
1 tbsp fresh thyme, chopped
1 tbsp chives, chopped
$3\frac{3}{4}$ cups chicken stock
$1\frac{1}{4}$ cups coconut milk, made with creamed coconut
1 hot chili
Salt and pepper

8 oz white crabmeat
3 crab claws, cracked

PREPARATION:
1. Wash the dasheen or spinach, drain well, and shred finely.

2. Melt the butter and oil in a large pan, add the onion and garlic, and cook over a moderate heat for 5 minutes. Stir in the okra and the herbs and cook for a further 5 minutes, stirring constantly.

3. Stir in the dasheen or spinach and cook for 3 minutes. Add the stock, coconut milk, chili and seasoning. Bring to a boil, then simmer, covered, for 15 minutes. Remove the chili and cook for a further 15 minutes.

4. If you wish, blend the soup very briefly, but do not overprocess. Return the soup to the pan, stir in the crabmeat and claws, and heat through for 5 minutes.

5. Serve warm or hot with a piece of crab-claw in each bowl.

CRAB BISQUE (right)

Crab, whether softshell, freshwater or spiny, is a strong favorite in Louisiana, and can be used to produce a deliciously rich soup, while corn is of course a traditional extra which is very popular throughout the whole of America. Most important, though, is to make a good stock first.

Serves 4

INGREDIENTS:
Stock:
Shells of 2 crabs (or 1 crab and lobster)
1 lb fresh shrimp or crawfish
1 large onion, quartered
1 peeled carrot
2 sticks of celery
Few bay leaves
Few black peppercorns
Water to cover (about 5 cups)
Juice of $\frac{1}{2}$ lemon
1–2 glasses of dry white wine
Parsley stalks
Salt

Bisque:
4 tbsp butter or sunflower oil
1 large onion, finely chopped
3 cloves of garlic, finely chopped
1 red or yellow pepper, seeded and finely chopped
2 sticks of celery, thinly sliced
$\frac{1}{2}$ cup flour
$3\frac{3}{4}$ cups good seafood or fish stock (Step 1.)
1 lb fresh crabmeat, taken from the body and claws
 and kept in chunks
$\frac{3}{4}$ cup heavy cream
Salt and pepper
Extra cream to serve

PREPARATION:
1. Place the first eight stock ingredients in a very large

pan. Bring to a boil and bubble gently for 30–40 minutes or until reduced by half. Add the lemon juice, wine, the parsley stalks, and salt to taste. Bring back to a boil and simmer for a further 15 minutes. Strain, and check the seasoning again before use.

2. Melt the butter in a large pan and gently cook the onion, garlic, peppers and celery until all have become soft but not browned.

3. Stir in the flour and blend until all the fat is absorbed. Cook for 1–2 minutes to form a thick roux.

4. Gradually add the stock, a little at a time, beating or whisking well to prevent lumps from forming. When all the stock is added, bring to a boil and simmer for 15 minutes.

5. Add the crabmeat chunks and simmer for a further 15 minutes, then blend or sieve the soup to produce a smooth finish.

6. Return to the pan, add the cream and seasonings to taste, and reheat without boiling. Serve topped with an extra swirl of cream.

VEGETABLE AND GREEN CHILI SOUP (below)

It is important to find mild green chilies, such as Anaheim, for this soup, as it is not meant to be seriously hot. The result should be a mellow spiciness combined with the unique taste of spinach.

Serves 4

INGREDIENTS:
1/2 cup butter
1 large red onion, chopped
2 cloves of garlic, finely chopped
2 medium potatoes, peeled and diced
1–2 carrots, peeled and sliced
5 cups chicken stock
1 cup mild green chilies, roasted and chopped
2/3 cup spinach, cooked and puréed
1/4 cup green beans, quartered
1/4 cup red kidney beans, cooked
1/4 cup black-eyed beans, cooked

8 tbsp light cream
4 tbsp Cheddar cheese or Monterey Jack, grated

PREPARATION:
1. In a large pan, heat the butter and sauté the onion and garlic until translucent. Add the potatoes and carrots and sauté for another 3–4 minutes.

2. Add the stock, chilies and spinach purée and bring to a boil. Simmer gently for about 10 minutes or until the potatoes and carrots are just tender.

3. Add the beans and cook for a further 5 minutes, then stir in the cream and heat through again gently.

4. Season to taste and serve topped with the cheese.

HOT PEPPER AND BEAN SOUP (right)

The characteristic smoky flavor of the beans is enhanced by the unusual addition of Madeira. Should a more mellow taste be required, paprika can be substituted for the Tabasco sauce.

Serves 4

INGREDIENTS:
1 cup red or brown beans, or a mixture of both, soaked overnight
2 tbsp butter
1 large onion, finely chopped
2 cloves of garlic, chopped
1 large leek, well washed and finely sliced
2 sticks of celery, diced
2 bay leaves
1 ham knuckle
1 red pepper, seeded and chopped
2 large tomatoes, seeded and chopped
1 tbsp tomato purée
Pinch of ground cloves
1 tbsp Tabasco sauce or paprika
Salt
4–5 tbsp Madeira wine
1 tbsp chopped cilantro or flat-leaf parsley

PREPARATION:
1. Place the soaked, drained beans in a large pan, cover with fresh water, bring to a boil, then simmer for 1–1½ hours or until almost tender. (Do not add salt at this stage or the beans will not soften.)

2. In another large pan, heat the butter and sauté the onion until translucent. Add the garlic, leek and celery and toss them over a high heat for a minute or so.

3. Add the bay leaves and the ham knuckle, adding sufficient water to cover. Bring to a boil and simmer, covered, for at least one hour, carefully spooning off any scum that rises to the surface. Discard the knuckle and strain.

4. Return the stock to the pan and add the drained beans, pepper, tomatoes, tomato purée, ground cloves, Tabasco, and salt to taste. Bring to a boil and simmer for a further 30–40 minutes or until the beans are quite tender.

5. Add the Madeira and cook for a couple of minutes. Check the seasoning and serve with a sprinkle of cilantro.

PIQUANT ALLIGATOR CHOWDER

Alligator meat has long been popular in Louisiana and the Mississippi area, even more so since it is now being successfully farmed. The taste of the firm white flesh lies somewhere between chicken and fish. If unobtainable, monkfish makes a good substitute.

Serves 4

INGREDIENTS:
2 tbsp butter or oil
1 large onion, sliced
2 sticks of celery, sliced
1 tbsp flour
$3^{3}/_{4}$ cups hot chicken stock
Few strands of saffron
2 large tomatoes, skinned, seeded and chopped
2 carrots, sliced
1 large potato, peeled and diced
1 pepper, seeded and chopped
1 tsp dried thyme
1 tsp salt
$^{1}/_{2}$ tsp black pepper
$^{1}/_{2}$–1 tsp cayenne
1 tsp crushed or chopped garlic
8–12 oz alligator meat, cut into large pieces

PREPARATION:
1. Heat the butter in a large pan and fry the onion and celery until translucent. Stir in the flour and cook to form a paste.

2. Gradually blend in the hot stock, stirring constantly as it comes to a boil to prevent lumps from forming. Add the saffron, tomatoes, carrots, potato, pepper, thyme, seasonings and garlic. Bring back to a boil and simmer gently for 10–15 minutes.

3. Add the meat and cook for about 30 minutes, stirring occasionally. Continue to simmer gently until the meat is tender. Check that the dish is salty enough before serving.

FRIED RICE BALLS WITH RED PEPPER SAUCE (right)

Rice plays an integral part in Louisiana farming and cooking. It is a feature of many a meal and any that is left over is always put to good use, either as sweet or savory offerings.

Serves 4

INGREDIENTS:
2 red peppers
2 tbsp butter
1 small onion, finely chopped
1 green chili, seeded and very finely chopped
2 scallions, very finely chopped
12 oz leftover cooked rice
Few saffron strands soaked in 1 tbsp boiling water
$^{1}/_{2}$ cup flour
Salt
1 tsp mustard powder
$^{1}/_{2}$ cup Cheddar cheese or Monterey Jack, finely grated
2–3 tbsp light vegetable stock
1–2 tsp Tabasco sauce
4 tbsp cornmeal
1 large egg, beaten
Oil for frying

PREPARATION:
1. Halve the peppers and roast them until they are blistered and blackened all over. Place them in a plastic bag and leave to cool.

2. Heat the butter in a small pan and sauté the onion until tender. Add the chili and scallions and cook for another 2 minutes.

3. Put the rice in a large bowl and mix in the onions and chili, the saffron and its liquid, 1 tablespoon of flour, salt, mustard and cheese. When thoroughly mixed, shape into about 20 balls. Chill.

4. Prepare the sauce by removing the skins from the roasted peppers. Process the flesh in a blender with the stock, seasoning and Tabasco sauce, adding extra stock, if necessary, to produce a light pouring consistency. Cover tightly and keep warm.

5. Mix the rest of the flour with the cornmeal and put it on a large plate, placing the beaten egg on another. Coat the rice balls with egg, drain off the excess, then coat in the flour and cornmeal mixture. Set aside when well coated, or repeat with any remaining mixture to give a crunchier crust.

6. When ready to serve, heat the oil in a deep-fat fryer to 350F. Shake off any excess coating from the balls

and fry three to four at a time for 2 minutes or until golden all over. Remove with a slotted spoon and drain on paper towels.

7. Transfer to a hot plate and keep warm while you cook the rest. Serve with the warm sauce.

Tip: Make smaller versions to serve as tasty bites for a cocktail party.

EGGS PAULETTE

This is just one of many ways to prepare artichokes in Louisiana. It's especially good if you are entertaining. Serve either as an appetizer or as part of a luxury brunch or light lunch.

11

Serves 8 as an appetizer or 4 for brunch

INGREDIENTS:

Artichokes:

6 medium globe artichokes
1 large lemon, cut into 4
2 cloves of garlic
3–4 tbsp olive oil
Salt and black pepper
2 tbsp butter
1 small onion, finely chopped
1–2 tsp Tabasco sauce

Hollandaise sauce:

2 large egg yolks, whisked
2 tsp white wine
3 tsp lemon juice
$\frac{1}{2}$ tsp Worcestershire sauce
1 cup butter, cubed
8 very small hen or quail eggs

PREPARATION:

1. Cut the bases from the artichokes with a stainless steel knife (to prevent discoloration), and discard any of the outer leaves which are damaged or tough. Fill a large pan with water, add the lemon; one clove of garlic, bruised; the oil; and 3–4 teaspoons of salt. Bring to a boil. Add the artichokes and boil gently, covered, until a leaf pulls out easily (20–25 minutes). Remove and drain well.

2. Set aside two artichokes. Cut the others in half vertically, then remove or pull out the chokes and the tiny purple-tinged leaves in the center, leaving the tender hearts visible. Keep warm, wrapped in aluminum foil, until ready to serve.

3. Place the hearts of the two reserved artichokes, together with the flesh scraped from the bases of the leaves, into a bowl. Protect with plastic wrap.

4. Heat 2 tablespoons of butter in a small heavy-based pan and cook the onions gently until translucent. Add the reserved artichoke flesh, mash or blend it well, then add Tabasco and the seasonings to taste. Spoon the mixture into the shells of the other 8 halves.

5. Place the egg yolks, the wine, lemon juice and Worcestershire sauce in a bowl set over a pan of simmering water, and whisk until pale and fluffy. Gradually add the cubed butter, whisking all the time as it melts, until the sauce is thick and glossy. Season to taste, cover with plastic wrap, and keep warm.

6. Lightly poach the hen or quail eggs and drain them well. Arrange the warm filled artichoke halves on serving plates or on one large platter. Place a poached egg on top of each one, then spoon over a little Hollandaise sauce. Serve with a salad garnish or a few crisply sautéed potatoes.

BARBECUED SHRIMP WITH SWEET PEPPER RÉMOULADE (opposite)

The classic rémoulade is predominantly a mustard sauce, based on mayonnaise with other additions such as gherkins and capers, and is the ideal accompaniment for eggs, fried and grilled fish, vegetables, and even cold meats. It can be stored for several days in a refrigerator and improves with keeping. This version has red peppers added for extra sweetness.

Serves 4

INGREDIENTS:

Sauce (makes 1$\frac{1}{4}$ cups):

2 tbsp tomato ketchup
1 clove of garlic, crushed
1–2 canned or bottled red peppers, chopped
2 tbsp chopped parsley
1 tbsp Creole or Dijon mustard
2 egg yolks
8 tbsp vegetable oil
1–2 tsp lemon juice
1 tsp white wine vinegar
1 tsp Tabasco sauce
1 tbsp Worcestershire sauce
1 tbsp paprika
1 tsp salt

Barbecued shrimp:

12 oz shrimp
Olive oil

PREPARATION:

1. In a blender, process the first 5 ingredients together to form a smooth paste. Beat the egg yolks in a small bowl with a balloon whisk until pale and creamy.

2. Slowly add the oil to the yolks in a fine stream until the mixture takes on the appearance of mayonnaise. Beat in the paste and the remaining sauce ingredients very gradually.

3. Season to taste and chill in an airtight container or a bottle with a lid.

4. Brush the shrimp with oil and barbecue or grill them for 2–3 minutes on each side. Serve immediately with the chilled sauce.

CHILI-BARBECUED SHRIMP (below)
These need only minutes on a barbecue and will disappear even quicker! Any large shrimp can be used, also crawfish and crab legs.

Serves 4 as a starter, or can be part of a barbecue selection

INGREDIENTS:
2 shallots, finely chopped
1 red chili, seeded and very thinly sliced or chopped
$1/2$ cup olive and sunflower oils, mixed
3–4 tbsp dry white wine
Salt to taste
1 lb large, peeled shrimp

PREPARATION:
1. Prepare a marinade by simmering the shallots and chili in a small pan with the oil, wine and seasoning. When the vegetables are tender, but not browned, pour into a large shallow dish to cool.

2. Wash and dry the shrimp, making a shallow cut along the back and deveining them, if necessary. Then put them in the marinade for an hour or so, turning them once or twice.

3. When ready to cook, remove the shrimp from the marinade and barbecue them for 1–2 minutes until they just turn pink. Baste with the marinade once or twice during the process and serve with a little more of the marinade poured over.

CRAB CAKES WITH FRESH CHILI SAUCE (right)
Prepare these the day before and cook them briefly at the last minute when you wish to serve them. These make a great appetizer or a light lunch with a salad; alternatively, they can be made bite-sized for a party buffet.

Makes 10–12

INGREDIENTS:
Crab cakes:
1 lb crabmeat (fresh, frozen or canned)
Salt and black pepper
1 tsp anchovy essence or a few drops of chili sauce
1 egg white
1 tbsp finely chopped parsley
1 tbsp chopped scallions (green parts only)
2 tbsp fine white breadcrumbs
2 tbsp flour
4 tbsp butter and a little oil for frying

Chili sauce:
3 cloves of garlic

1 hot red chili or 1 large mild green chili, seeded
2 very large tomatoes, seeded
2 tbsp chopped cilantro, mint and parsley, mixed
Juice of 1 lime
2–3 tbsp olive oil

PREPARATION:
1. In a large bowl, mix the crab with the seasonings, egg white, herbs and breadcrumbs. Combine together very thoroughly. Chill well.

2. Divide the mixture into 10–12 small cakes, dusting each one lightly with flour.

3. Mix all the sauce ingredients together, with salt and pepper to taste, or they can be blended in a food processor. Chill until required.

4. Heat half the butter and oil until they bubble and cook half the fish cakes, basting and turning them frequently until they are golden all over (6–7 minutes altogether). Transfer to paper towels to drain while you cook the remainder. Serve hot with green vegetables and the chili sauce.

DEVILED CRAB
The large meaty Blue crab, obtainable at the height of the season when it is most plentiful, is perfect for this delicious dish. It needs to be well spiked with Tabasco sauce and is good served warm or cold.

Serves 4

INGREDIENTS:
2 sticks of celery, finely chopped
1 green pepper, finely chopped
3–4 scallions, finely chopped
2–3 tbsp chopped parsley
1 lb fresh crabmeat, flaked
1–2 tsp salt
1 tsp mustard
Tabasco sauce to taste
5–6 tbsp heavy cream
6 tbsp melted butter
$^3/_4$ cup fresh white breadcrumbs

PREPARATION:
1. In a large bowl, mix together the celery, pepper, scallions, parsley, crabmeat, salt, mustard, Tabasco, cream and half the butter until well blended.

2. Preheat the oven to 350F. Spoon the mixture into a gratin dish and sprinkle on the breadcrumbs. Spoon the remaining melted butter over and bake for 20–30 minutes until the top is golden. Serve with fresh bread and a salad garnish.

OYSTER BROCHETTES
For oyster lovers, this is an experience not to be missed. The brochettes are traditionally served on a bed of rice.

Serves 4

INGREDIENTS:
$^1/_2$ tsp each salt and celery salt
1 tsp each white and black pepper and cayenne
$^1/_2$ tsp chopped dried oregano
8 oz lean bacon, rinds removed and cut into pieces
40 oysters, freshly shucked (reserve the juice)
$^1/_2$ cup cornmeal
Oil for frying
$^1/_2$ cup butter
1 clove of garlic, crushed
1 tbsp finely chopped parsley

PREPARATION:
1. Soak 8 fine wooden skewers in water to prevent them from burning. Mix together the seasonings and the oregano.

2. Arrange the bacon and oysters alternately on the skewers.

3. Mix the seasoning mixture and the cornmeal together and dip the skewers in this to coat them well.

4. Heat 2–3 tbsp oil and butter in a frying pan and fry 3–4 brochettes at a time until they are golden. Drain on paper towels and keep warm while cooking the rest.

5. Heat the remaining butter with the garlic and cook gently for a few minutes to flavor the butter. Discard the garlic and serve the brochettes with the butter poured over and sprinkled with parsley.

OYSTERS WITH CHAMPAGNE AND CAVIAR (right)
This is a dish for special occasions when a little luxury is in order. You can do little in the way of advance preparation except to make the first two stages of the sauce; everything else can only be done at the last minute.

Serves 4

INGREDIENTS:
2 tbsp finely chopped shallots
Small glass of champagne or chablis
Pinch of salt
1 tbsp white wine vinegar
$^1/_2$ cup unsalted butter (at room temperature)
24 oysters
Lemon wedges
4 tbsp caviar or lumpfish roe
Coarse rock salt

PREPARATION:
1. In a small pan, mix together the shallots, wine, salt and vinegar. Bring to a boil and cook gently until the liquid has reduced to about 2 tablespoons.

2. Whisk in the butter, in small lumps, until you have a creamy sauce. Cover the sauce to prevent a skin from forming.

3. Shuck the oysters, then strain their juices through fine cheesecloth into the sauce. Return the oysters to their cleaned, deeper half-shells, and place them on plates of rock salt with lemon wedges.

4. To serve, reheat the butter sauce gently, whisking it constantly, then sieve it and pour a teaspoonful over each oyster. Top each one with $^1/_2$ teaspoon of caviar and serve as soon as possible accompanied by a glass of champagne or chablis.

BRUNCHES & SANDWICHES

ZESTY EGG AND BEAN BRUNCH

This makes an unusual but easy weekend brunch as the tomato and bean mixture can be made the day before and reheated.

Serves 4

INGREDIENTS:
1 tbsp vegetable oil
1 onion, diced
14 oz chopped canned tomatoes
14 oz canned red kidney beans, drained and rinsed
1½ tsp chili powder
Salt
4 eggs

Garnish:
6–8 crisp lettuce leaves, shredded
Corn chips

PREPARATION:
1. Heat the oil in a very large skillet and fry the onion over a medium heat until soft, stirring all the while.

2. Stir in the tomatoes and their juice, add the kidney beans, chili powder and salt. Bring to a boil, then cook over a moderate heat, stirring occasionally, until the mixture slightly reduces and becomes thick.

3. Using a spoon, make 4 deep indentations in the tomato mixture. Break the eggs, one at a time, into a small bowl and slip them into the hollows.

4. Cover the pan with a lid and cook gently for 8–10 minutes until the eggs set.

5. Divide the lettuce between 4 serving plates, then spoon the tomato mixture on top, being careful not to disturb the eggs. Serve with corn chips.

OYSTER OMELET (right)

Louisianans love oysters any way at all, but for a luxurious appetizer, brunch or light lunch, this omelet surely beats all. Be sure, of course, that the oysters are fresh and are used as soon as possible. Buy them still in their shells and packed with as much of their juice as possible.

Serves 1–2

MARDI GRAS EGGS (above)

Just one of many ways to serve eggs for brunch; but for the finishing touch, serve or top each egg with a spoonful of warm Hollandaise sauce (page 13).

INGREDIENTS PER PERSON:
½ fresh English muffin, toasted and buttered
1 large tomato, sliced and lightly broiled
2 slices of bacon, rinds removed and broiled (one crisply)
1 egg, poached
Parsley or chervil
Freshly ground black pepper

PREPARATION:
1. Place the warm muffin on a hot plate, top with a tomato slice and a slice of lightly cooked bacon.

2. Top with a softly-poached egg and the other slice of bacon, crisply cooked and crumbled, plus a sprinkling of black pepper and a herb garnish.

INGREDIENTS:

6 fresh oysters in their shells
Lemon juice
3 medium to large fresh eggs
Salt and black pepper
1 tbsp butter

PREPARATION:

1. Shuck the oysters and strain their juice into a small bowl. Squeeze a little lemon juice over the oysters and roughly chop them up.

2. Thoroughly beat 3 eggs together with a little seasoning. Heat half the butter in a heavy-based omelet pan and pour in the eggs. Stir, drawing the edges into the middle of the omelet with a fork, until the base is just set.

3. Spoon the oysters onto one half of the omelet and fold it over. Still over a gentle heat, spoon any oyster juice over the omelet, allowing no more than a further 1 minute of cooking time. Serve immediately with thin brown bread and butter.

BACON AND PECAN MUFFINS

Muffins are perfect for an easy breakfast, brunch or light lunch. Make them in advance, then store them overnight or freeze them for a longer period. Reheat them when required.

Makes 8

INGREDIENTS:

1 cup all-purpose flour
1 cup cornmeal or polenta
2 tsp baking powder
2 eggs, beaten
4 tbsp butter, melted and slightly cooled
1 tbsp maple syrup
1 cup milk
$2/3$ cup pecan nuts, finely chopped
8 slices of bacon, lightly broiled and chopped
Ground black pepper
4 tbsp Parmesan cheese, grated

PREPARATION:

1. Mix the flour, cornmeal and baking powder together. Beat in the eggs, butter, maple syrup and milk, and when well mixed, stir in the nuts, bacon and a little pepper. Leave to stand for 10 minutes.

2. Preheat the oven to 375F.

3. Spoon the mixture into 8 lightly greased deep muffin cups and sprinkle on the cheese. Bake for 10–12 minutes until well risen and golden.

4. Serve warm with butter or a bowl of crème fraîche or fromage frais.

APPLE AND CINNAMON MUFFINS (overleaf left)

These quick and simple-to-make muffins are delicious for breakfast or brunch. If you make them the day before, don't refrigerate them but store them in an airtight container, returning them to a hot oven for 5 minutes before serving.

Makes 10–12

INGREDIENTS:

2 cups all-purpose flour
$1/2$ tsp salt
1 tsp ground cinnamon

3 tbsp superfine sugar
2 eggs, beaten
Scant cup milk
4 tbsp butter, melted
1 large sweet apple, skinned, cored and diced
4 tbsp raisins

PREPARATION:
1. Preheat the oven to 375F. Lightly grease a 12-muffin pan, or use muffin cups and place them on cookie sheets ready for filling.

2. Sift the flour, salt and cinnamon into a bowl and add the sugar. Beat the eggs, milk and melted butter together, then stir into the dry ingredients. Add the diced apple and raisins and stir in lightly.

3. Divide the mixture up and bake for 30 minutes or until well risen and just firm to the touch. Serve warm with melted butter or cold with ice cream or crème fraîche.

BANANA BREAD (above)
A great treat, this bread becomes even moister when kept for a day or two, though this is easier said than done in the face of such temptation.

Serves 6–8

INGREDIENTS:
$^3/_4$ cup butter or margarine
Scant cup light brown sugar
Few drops of vanilla extract
1 tbsp lemon juice
3 bananas, mashed
3 eggs, beaten
2 cups all-purpose flour, sifted
1 tsp baking powder
$^1/_3$ cup currants or raisins

PREPARATION:
1. Cream the butter and sugar together until the mixture is light and fluffy. Combine the vanilla extract

with the lemon juice and bananas, then blend them into the butter and sugar mixture. Preheat oven to 325F.

2. Gradually fold in the beaten eggs, alternating them with the flour mixed with the baking powder, then add the currants or raisins. When blended, spoon into a greased 2-lb loaf pan or 8-inch lined cake pan.

3. Bake in a loaf pan for about 1 hour or until firm to the touch. Cool in the pan before turning out.

BACON AND MUSHROOM RICE (below)

This is not unlike a risotto, though it is less time-consuming to prepare. It is a most accommodating dish, ideal not only for late risers but also for late arrivals!

Serves 4

INGREDIENTS:
2 tbsp sunflower oil
1 large onion chopped
1 large clove of garlic, crushed (optional)
6 oz bacon, rinds removed and chopped
6 oz button mushrooms
1½ cups American long-grain rice
½ cup wild rice
3 cups chicken or vegetable stock

2 tbsp lemon juice
Ground black pepper
Chives

PREPARATION:
1. In a large pan, heat the oil and gently fry the onion, garlic and bacon for 2 minutes. Add the mushrooms and sauté, stirring frequently, until the bacon is cooked through.

2. Transfer the bacon and mushrooms to another dish, add the rice to the pan, and fry for one minute, stirring briskly. Add the stock, bring to a boil, then simmer, covered, for 10 minutes or until the rice is nearly tender.

3. Return the bacon and mushrooms to the pan, add the lemon juice and black pepper, and extra stock if necessary. Heat through, or continue cooking until the rice is just tender. Sprinkle with chives and serve with triangles of toast and a tomato salad.

Tip: You could cook this dish the day or evening before, ready to reheat gently in the oven or in the microwave. It would also freeze well, then left to defrost overnight and reheated slowly in the oven covered with aluminum foil.

FAJITAS (left)

Little known outside Texas until quite recently, like so many other snacks fajitas have traveled well and are now popular throughout the South. They would originally have been made with beef, but strips of chicken, or even vegetables, with a piquant sauce and plenty of cheese, are equally as delicious.

Serves 4

INGREDIENTS:
Fajitas:
2 tbsp olive oil
12 oz chicken fillets, cut into thin strips
2 tbsp fresh lemon juice
1 clove of garlic, crushed or sliced
$\frac{1}{2}$ each red and green peppers
$\frac{1}{2}$ red chili, seeded and chopped
2 tbsp guacamole dip or spread
2 tbsp tomato sauce
4 soft flour tortilla wraps

Sauce:
$1\frac{1}{4}$ cups milk
1 tbsp butter
1 tbsp cornstarch
2 tsp mustard
Salt
$\frac{1}{2}$ tsp each black and red pepper
1 cup grated Cheddar cheese or Monterey Jack

PREPARATION:
1. Heat the oil in a pan and sauté the strips of chicken with the lemon juice and garlic until just firm. Add the peppers and chili. Remove and keep warm.

2. Heat the milk with the butter and whisk in the cornstarch and mustard. Continue whisking as the sauce begins to boil and thicken to prevent lumps from forming. Continue cooking, whisking, for 1–2 minutes.

3. Add the seasonings to the sauce and cook for 2 minutes. Remove from the heat and add the cheese, mixing well. Allow to cool slightly.

4. Spread the tomato sauce over the base of an ovenproof dish. Divide the chicken, peppers, chili, and guacamole between the tortillas and cover with the cheese sauce. Roll them up and place them in the dish. Sprinkle with more cheese, and place under a hot broiler for 3–4 minutes until the top is lightly brown.

COUSH COUSH

This old-fashioned but popular family breakfast or brunch dish is similar to Scottish porridge, but instead of oatmeal it is made with cornmeal. Serve it with milk or cream and syrup for a hearty start to a cold winter's day.

Serves 4

INGREDIENTS:
$1\frac{1}{3}$ cups yellow cornmeal
$\frac{1}{2}$–1 tsp salt
1 tsp baking powder
$\frac{3}{4}$ cup milk
$\frac{3}{4}$ cup water
3 tbsp sunflower oil
Corn or maple syrup or light brown sugar
Heavy cream

PREPARATION:
1. Mix the first three dry ingredients together, then beat in the milk and water until blended to a smooth batter.

2. Heat the oil in a heavy-based pan and when quite hot pour in the batter and allow a crust to form underneath.

3. Reduce the heat and stir occasionally while cooking for 10–15 minutes until you have a thick porridge-like consistency.

4. Serve portions topped with syrup or sugar and cream

Tip: If you prefer, you can bake this in the oven at 325F for about 1 hour. Stir occasionally and finish off with a knob of butter before serving.

HUSH PUPPIES

These are battered corn fritters that are traditionally served with fried fish. They can be flavored with cheese, onions, spices, or even pecans.

Makes about 20

INGREDIENTS:
3 oz corn kernels, canned or frozen
$\frac{2}{3}$ cup all-purpose flour

3. Heat two inches of oil in a deep frying pan, or use a deep-fryer with the correct amount of oil heated to 350F. Carefully drop small spoonfuls of the mixture into the pan and cook a few at a time, so that there is plenty of space for them to move around, until golden brown.

4. Remove with a slotted spoon and drain on paper towels. Serve sprinkled with a little salt.

MUFFULETTA (left)

You could call it a sandwich but this Italian invader is frequently dinner-plate-sized! Made from a variety of cold cuts, garlicky marinated vegetables, and layers of creamy cheese, it is a meal with attitude. However, it must be well pressed and the flavors given time to develop. Some even say that when taking a recently made muffuletta on a pinic, you should sit on it (well wrapped of course) for part of the journey, so that the rich olive-oil juices can mingle evenly throughout the layers of filling.

Serves 3 or 4

INGREDIENTS:
1 large, round white loaf of Italian or French bread, sliced through the middle
Slices of cold cooked or cured meats or salamis
A selection of antipasti or prepared salads (marinated peppers, olives in garlic and oil, wild mushrooms in vinaigrette, pickles, etc.)
Thick slices of fresh mozzarella
Extra olive oil

PREPARATION:
1. Remove most of the soft inner part of the bread, creating a cavity within each half. Brush the cavities with olive oil, then layer them up with as many of the various fillings as possible, plus all the juices or flavored oils from the ingredients. Sprinkle with seasoning, and pour on a little extra oil to finish.

2. Place the two halves together, then wrap the loaf tightly in plastic wrap. Place between two plates, putting weights on top so that the loaf is pressed down as much as possible. Refrigerate for at least an hour.

3. To serve, unwrap and cut into thick wedges.

$1^{1}/_{3}$ cup cornmeal
2 tsp baking powder
$^{1}/_{2}$ tsp each black pepper and cayenne
$^{1}/_{2}$–1 tsp salt
$^{1}/_{4}$ tsp each dried thyme and oregano
2 cloves of garlic, crushed
1 egg, beaten
1 cup milk, buttermilk or thin yogurt
Oil for frying

PREPARATION:
1. In a large bowl, mix together the corn and all the dry ingredients.

2. In a separate bowl, mix together the garlic, egg and milk. Stir this gently into the dry ingredients until lightly blended.

PO'BOYS

What makes a po'boy special is the bread – a po'boy just isn't the genuine article unless it's made with good-quality, fresh French bread, and the kind made in New Orleans is just right, with a crunchy crust and a very light center. The loaves are about 3-foot-long, and about 6 inches in circumference.

Po'boy is, of course, short for "poor boy," which suggests a cheap, filling street food, eaten on the move, and it is best regarded as such. Consequently, the least expensive po'boys on the menu will almost always contain the cheapest ingredients, and might include pressed meats, Italian sausage or French fries. French fries? You betcha! In fact, with a little roast beef gravy added, they make a wonderful treat; to watch guys in suits devouring them, while standing around in groups, may make you wonder what is wrong with this picture, and you won't understand until you try one for yourself.

Po'boys made with hot roast beef smothered with gravy, with shredded lettuce, tomatoes and mayonnaise, or oysters coated in cornmeal, deep-fried and covered with tartar sauce, are the most popular fillings, but just about anything that can be put inside French bread will taste good, as long as fresh, quality ingredients are used. Fried catfish is steadily growing in popularity, while the recipe below would turn the po'boy into a thing of elegance.

Many establishments do excellent ready-prepared hamburger or cheeseburger po'boys, which can be quickly cooked to order, but it is a different story when it comes to roast beef and ham, which are better freshly cooked on the premises. Nowadays, however, proprietors of most lunch counters seldom home-cook their own meats, making the ones that do all the more desirable.

The move towards healthier eating has led to such things as chicken breasts being added to the menu; but the rich combination of ingredients that makes a po-boy great just don't work as low-fat versions, so it is probably better to not even try!

NEW ORLEANS PO'BOY

Serves 4

INGREDIENTS:
4 large pieces of French bread
¾ cup pepper jelly
1 lb smoked duck breast, very thinly sliced

Cashew butter:
1 cup chopped cashews
¼ cup chopped peanuts
3 tbsp honey
1 tbsp molasses
Pinch of salt
½ cup softened butter

Red onion salad:
2 small red onions, finely sliced into rings
3 tbp sherry vinegar
3 tbsp olive oil
Salt and freshly ground pepper

Apple salad:
1 green dessert apple
1 celery heart
1 shallot, very finely chopped
2 tbsp olive oil
2 tbsp walnut vinegar
Pinch of salt

PREPARATION:
1. Roast the cashews and peanuts in an oven which has been preheated to 350F for about 6–8 minutes until they smell fragrant, then finely chop them in a blender with the honey, molasses and salt. Add the softened butter and blend to a "peanut butter" consistency.

2. Season the onions with salt and pepper, then sauté them in a little oil until barely tender. While still hot, marinate the onions in the vinegar and olive oil, season, and leave to cool.

3. Peel, core and slice the apple very thinly. Thinly slice the celery heart diagonally, then toss them with the shallot, oil, vinegar and salt.

4. When ready to assemble the sandwiches, preheat the oven to 400F and heat the duck meat and onion salad together until sizzling hot. Split the pieces of French bread into two and toast them very lightly until barely colored on both sides. Spread one half of each with the softened cashew butter and the other half with the pepper jelly. Divide the meat and onions between the four sandwiches and serve with the apple salad.

MEAT & POULTRY ENTRÉES

SPICY SOUTHERN FRIED CHICKEN (below)
This famous dish is hard to beat, so make plenty of the seasoning mix and store it away ready to use when the need arises.

Serves 4

INGREDIENTS:
8–10 small chicken portions
1 tbsp paprika
1 tbsp celery salt
1 tbsp onion powder
1 tbsp mustard powder
1 tsp cayenne
Salt
Freshly ground black pepper
1 tbsp flour
1 egg
3 tbsp water
Oil for deep frying

PREPARATION:
1. Wash the chicken portions and dry them carefully on paper towels. Place on a large tray.

2. Mix all the seasonings together, adding plenty of salt and black pepper, and finally the flour.

3. Thoroughly beat the egg with the water in a shallow bowl. Dip the chicken portions into the egg, then into the seasoning mixture, coating them thoroughly. Return them to the tray and leave them in the refrigerator to firm up slightly.

4. Meanwhile, heat the oil in a deep-fryer to 350F. Fry the chicken in batches, turning the portions carefully once or twice until evenly browned all over. They will need 6–8 minutes, but make sure they are well cooked through. If they appear to be browning too quickly, slightly reduce the heat in the fryer, if necessary removing the chicken from the fat while it cools down.

5. Drain the portions on kitchen paper and serve with rice or fries and a salad.

CHICKEN AND CORN PAN FRY (right)
This dish is quick and easy to prepare. Instead of initially frying them, the chicken portions could be cooked on a barbecue for extra flavor.

Serves 4

INGREDIENTS:
4 tbsp vegetable oil
8 chicken drumsticks or other small chicken portions
4 tbsp red or white wine
4 tbsp chicken stock
2 thick bacon slices, rinds removed and cut into strips
1 large red onion, sliced
2 cloves of garlic, chopped
1 large red or green pepper, seeded and sliced
1 large tomato, chopped
4 tbsp sweetcorn kernels
Salt and pepper

PREPARATION:
1. Heat the oil in a large wok or frying pan, add the chicken, then fry for 10–12 minutes until golden brown.

2. Pour the wine and stock over the chicken and cook for 10 minutes until tender.

3. Stir in the bacon, onion, garlic and pepper and cook for a further 5–6 minutes.

4. Add the tomato and sweetcorn and season with salt and pepper. Continue cooking for 5 minutes until the vegetables are tender. Serve immediately.

CHICKEN ÉTOUFFÉE (overleaf)
To cook à l'étouffée *is to braise meat in a small amount of liquid but smothered in aromatic vegetables which give flavor and added moisture to the dish. In Cajun cooking, the method involves making a thick roux-based sauce first.*

Serves 4

INGREDIENTS:
$^1/_3$ cup flour
6 tbsp peanut or vegetable oil
3 lb chicken, cut into quarters
4 tbsp butter
9 oz onions, chopped
3 scallions, chopped
2 sticks of celery, cut into large pieces
4 green chilis, seeded and chopped
1 lb fresh tomatoes, skinned, seeded and chopped
$2^1/_2$ cups chicken stock

27

1 tsp chopped fresh thyme
1 bay leaf
Salt and pepper
1 red onion, chopped
1¼ cups American long-grain rice
2¼ cups water
1 tbsp fresh parsley, chopped

PREPARATION:
1. Put the flour into a heavy-based pan. Gradually add 4 tablespoons of oil and mix to a smooth paste. Cook the roux over a moderate heat, stirring constantly for 15–20 minutes until it has turned a deep golden brown.

2. Cook the chicken pieces in the remaining oil in a deep frying pan for 20 minutes until golden brown and cooked through.

3. Melt half the butter in another frying pan. Fry the onions and scallions for 5–7 minutes until soft, add the celery and cook for 2 minutes. Add the chilis and cook for 2 more minutes, then stir in the tomatoes and cook for another 5 minutes.

4. Stir in the roux, mixing well to prevent lumps from forming. Mix in the chicken stock and herbs and season well with salt and pepper. Cover and simmer for 20 minutes.

5. Meanwhile, melt the remaining butter in a pan, add the red onion and cook for 2 minutes. Stir in the rice, cook for a minute, then pour over the water. Add seasoning and bring to a boil. Simmer for 15 minutes until the rice is tender and the liquid is absorbed.

6. Stir the parsley into the rice and put it into a serving dish, then spoon the chicken and sauce over the rice. Serve immediately.

CHICKEN GUMBO FILÉ (right)

Main-course gumbos are a one-pot meal. Throw in anything you have that day in the refrigerator that seems suitable, such as ham or ham bones, andouille or other sausages, leftover turkey, duck or goose, or even game such as venison, rabbit or hare.

Serves 6

INGREDIENTS:
2 lb chicken
2 tsp salt
4 tbsp butter or oil
2 onions, chopped
2 peppers, seeded and chopped
2 sticks of celery, chopped
2 cloves of garlic, chopped
Bay leaves
8 oz okra, sliced
1 tsp each cayenne, black pepper and filé powder
1–2 tbsp chopped scallions

PREPARATION:
1. Place the chicken in a large pan and cover it with water. Add salt and bring to a boil, then simmer gently for about 40 minutes or until the chicken is thoroughly cooked. Reserve the stock. Cut the chicken into pieces.

2. In a separate pan, melt the butter and cook the onions, peppers and celery until soft. Add the chicken, garlic, bay leaves, okra and seasonings and stir over a gentle heat for 3–4 minutes.

3. Add the chicken stock gradually, then bring to a boil, cover, and simmer gently for 30–40 minutes, stirring occasionally.

4. When the gumbo is ready it should be rich, thick, and well seasoned. If it has not thickened sufficiently,

remove the lid and continue to cook a little longer. Sprinkle with the scallions and serve over rice or with rice on the side.

BAKED ACORN SQUASH STUFFED WITH FRAGRANT CHICKEN IN TOMATO SAUCE (overleaf left)

There are many types of squashes and pumpkins which can be used in this way. Take your pick and enjoy their soft, rich, buttery flavors. The filling for this dish can be made the day before and stored in the refrigerator overnight.

Serves: 6

INGREDIENTS:
6 small acorn squash
6 chicken breasts, trimmed and diced
Salt and pepper
2 tbsp vegetable oil
2 medium onions, finely diced
2 cloves of garlic, crushed
6 cardamom pods, crushed
14 oz canned chopped tomatoes
Finely grated rind of 2 lemons
$1\frac{1}{4}$ cups heavy cream
2 tbsp fresh parsley, chopped

PREPARATION:

1. Preheat the oven to 350F.

2. Cut a lid off the top of each squash and trim their bases so that they sit upright.

3. Season the chicken with salt and pepper. Heat the oil in a skillet and quickly brown the chicken for 5 minutes. Remove, using a slotted spoon.

4. Add the onion, garlic and cardamon pods to the pan. Cook for a further 5–7 minutes. Stir in the tomatoes and lemon rind and season with salt and pepper.

5. Bring to a boil, add the chicken, and cook, uncovered, for 10 minutes or until the sauce thickens. Stir in the cream and parsley.

6. Fill each squash with the chicken mixture, top with their lids, then put them into a lightly greased ovenproof dish. Bake for 30 minutes.

7. When the squashes are tender throughout, serve with savory rice and a crisp salad.

BOUDIN BLANC IN SPICY TOMATO SAUCE (above)

The original boudin blanc is a French sausage made from a blend of poultry, veal or pork, very finely ground and lightly seasoned. It can be bound with eggs and cream, or just breadcrumbs, and piped into natural casings. It is then gently poached and served with a variety of sauces. New Orleans is famous for its boudins, which are likely to be made with pure pork, bound with rice, spiced with green peppers and onions, and highly flavored with cayenne and black pepper. Any similar unsmoked sausage can be substituted.

Serves 4

INGREDIENTS:

4 boudins blancs
3 tbsp sunflower or vegetable oil
1 large onion, sliced
2 sticks of celery, chopped
2 cloves of garlic, crushed
14 oz canned chopped tomatoes
1 tsp Tabasco or hot pepper sauce
1 tsp sugar
Salt and black pepper

PREPARATION:

1. Preheat the oven to 180F. Place the sausages in an ovenproof dish or small roasting pan and pour boiling water over them. Place in the oven and bake for 40 minutes, basting occasionally.

2. Meanwhile, make the sauce. Heat the oil in a medium-sized pan and sauté the onion, celery and garlic until translucent. Add the tomatoes, Tabasco sauce, sugar and seasoning, and simmer gently for about 15 minutes or until the mixture becomes thick and the flavors have melded. Sieve to give a smooth sauce and return it to a clean pan to warm through.

3. Remove the sausages from the water, leaving them to drain and cool slightly. Serve warm with the tomato sauce and rice or vegetables.

SAUSAGE WITH PASTA (right)

New Orleans andouille, served with pasta in a spicy sauce and well coated with a tangy honey dressing, make a delicious and quick supper.

Serves 4

INGREDIENTS:
12 oz fresh pasta
6 oz button mushrooms, halved
8 oz andouille or other pork sausages, sliced
2–3 tbsp olive oil
³/₄ cup chicken stock
4–5 tbsp heavy cream
1 tsp mustard
1 tsp Cajun or Creole seasoning
1 tsp paprika
Pinch of salt
2 tbsp chopped chives

PREPARATION:
1. Cook the pasta for 3–4 minutes in boiling water, then drain, leaving a little of the water still adhering to it.

2. Cook the mushrooms and sausage in the oil for 3–4 minutes until the sausage is evenly colored all over, stirring frequently to prevent sticking.

3. Add the stock, cream and seasonings and cook for a further 3 minutes until the flavors have had time to blend.

4. Return the pasta to the pan and stir to coat it lightly in the sauce. Cook briskly for 3–4 minutes, then sprinkle with the chives. Serve with a salad.

Tip: If you use dried pasta you will only need 6 ounces. Cook for 12–15 minutes, or as directed. You can use any shape of pasta, but more substantial types such as penne or shells suit the dish better.

ANDOUILLE AND LIMA BEAN SUPPER (overleaf)

This simple dish of sausage and beans uses canned beans. It is therefore a good standby and can be produced at a moment's notice.

Serves 3–4

INGREDIENTS:
2–3 tbsp olive oil
1 small onion, finely chopped
2 cloves of garlic, crushed

4 andouille or other sausage, thinly sliced
1 small glass of beer
14 oz canned lima beans, drained
2 tbsp chopped parsley
Salt and black pepper

PREPARATION:
1. Heat the oil in a heavy-based pan, then add the onion and garlic and fry until soft but not brown.

2. Add the sausage and cook over a high heat, stirring frequently until it has browned all over. Add the beer, the beans, half the parsley, and seasoning to taste.

3. Bring to a gentle bubble and heat through before sprinkling with the rest of the parsley and serving with fresh crusty bread and salad accompaniments.

CREOLE HOT SAUSAGES WITH SWEET PEPPERS AND WINE (right)
This is an interesting though fiery dish which can be served with a mixed salad or baked potatoes.

Serves 4

INGREDIENTS:
1 lb chorizo sausages
2 tbsp vegetable oil
$^3/_4$ cup chicken stock
1 large red onion, sliced
1 thick slice of ham, chopped
2 red peppers, seeded and chopped
1 large glass of white wine
Salt and pepper
2 slices of bread, cut into triangles (optional)

PREPARATION:
1. Preheat the oven to 350F.

2. Fry the sausages in 1 tablespoon of oil until lightly browned. Transfer to an ovenproof dish, pour over the stock, then cook in the oven for 15–20 minutes.

3. Meanwhile, heat another tablespoon of oil in a pan and fry the onion, ham and peppers for 4–5 minutes until tender. Pour over the wine and season well, then increase the heat to reduce the wine a little.

4. Place the sausages on a serving dish, spoon the onions and pepper mixture over. To garnish, triangles of fried bread can be arranged around the edges.

BEEF PEPPERPOT (overleaf)
In this dish, a less expensive cut of beef is used to produce a rich daube or stew – dark and spicy and with a touch of sweetness.

Serves 4

INGREDIENTS:
$1^1/_4$ lb lean braising steak
1–2 tbsp sunflower oil
1 large onion sliced, or 8 tiny onions halved
1 large clove of garlic, crushed

Serves 4

INGREDIENTS:

Grillades:
1 tsp salt
$\frac{1}{2}$ tsp cayenne
$\frac{1}{2}$ tsp black pepper
$\frac{1}{2}$ tsp white pepper
$\frac{1}{2}$ tsp mustard powder
1 tsp dried thyme
$\frac{1}{2}$ tsp filé gumbo powder
2 tbsp flour
4 thick pork chops or beef steaks
2 tbsp oil
2 tbsp butter
1 large onion, chopped
1 red pepper, seeded and chopped
2 sticks of celery, sliced
2 large cloves of garlic, crushed
1 cup rich beef stock or consommé
$\frac{1}{2}$ cup good tomato sauce
2 bay leaves

Grits:
$\frac{1}{2}$ cup grits
1 onion, finely chopped
$2\frac{1}{2}$ cups water or vegetable stock
2 large cloves of garlic, crushed
1 tbsp fresh chopped parsley or thyme to serve

PREPARATION:

1. Mix together the first seven ingredients. Reserve two teaspoons. Mix the rest with the flour, then coat the meat thoroughly in this seasoned mixture.

2. Heat the oil in a large pan and fry the chops or steaks for 3–4 minutes on both sides until nearly cooked. Remove and transfer to an ovenproof dish.

3. Add the butter to the pan, then stir in the onion, pepper, celery and garlic. Cook gently until brown, then stir in the stock and tomato sauce. Add the bay leaves and bring to a boil, stirring once or twice.

4. Return the meat to the pan and continue cooking, covered, until it is tender and the sauce is rich and has thickened.

5. Meanwhile, soak the grits in cold water for 10–15

1–2 tsp hot pepper sauce
$1\frac{1}{4}$ cups beef stock
2 tsp dark brown sugar
3 tbsp clear honey
1 tsp dried thyme
Salt
$\frac{1}{2}$ yellow pepper, sliced

PREPARATION:

1. Trim and chop or cube the meat. Fry in hot oil, a few pieces at a time, until browned all over. Add the onion and garlic and cook for a further 1–2 minutes.

2. Add the pepper sauce, stock, sugar, honey, thyme and salt. Cover, and simmer gently for 45–50 minutes, stirring occasionally until the meat is tender. Add the sliced pepper for the last 10–15 minutes. Serve with rice and baked yams.

GRILLADES AND GRITS

Grits are dried corn (hominy), ground to a fine texture and cooked to something like a porridge. However, they are very bland and need lots of flavorings. In this popular combination, they are served with tender slow-cooked meat bathed in a rich sauce.

minutes, then drain through a sieve. Place in a pan with the remaining ingredients (apart from the herbs) and bring to a good boil. Boil for 2–3 minutes, then simmer gently for 20–30 minutes, stirring occasionally.

6. When the grits are ready, serve sprinkled with the herbs, accompanied by the meat in its rich sauce.

JAMBALAYA (below)
This is a true Cajun dish from the heart of Louisiana and a perfect way of transforming leftovers into a hearty family meal.

Serves 4

INGREDIENTS:
2 tbsp vegetable oil

1 large onion, chopped
3 sticks of celery, chopped
1 green pepper, seeded and chopped
2 cloves of garlic, crushed
8 oz andouille or other sausage, sliced
2½ cups chicken stock
1¼ cups American long-grain rice
½ tsp cayenne
2 large tomatoes, skinned and chopped
8 oz cooked shrimp, peeled
8 oz cooked chicken, chopped

PREPARATION:
1. Heat the oil in a large pan and add the onion, celery, pepper and garlic. Cover with a lid and cook

over a low heat for 10–15 minutes until soft.

2. Add the sausage and cook for 2 minutes. Stir in the stock, rice, cayenne and tomatoes. Bring to a boil, cover with a lid, then simmer for 12–15 minutes until the rice is tender and the stock has been absorbed.

3. Stir in the shrimp and chicken and cook over a low heat until the chicken is heated through.

4. Spoon the jambalaya into a large dish and serve immediately.

DUCK BREASTS WITH ORANGE AND RUM (below)
This is reminiscent of the famous French canard à l'orange*, but with a New World addition of a slug or two of rum!*

Serves: 4

INGREDIENTS:
2 oranges
5 tbsp butter
2 ducks, portioned into breasts and thighs
3–4 tbsp rich duck stock or chicken consommé
3–4 tbsp rum
Salt and black pepper

PREPARATION:
1. Carefully remove the rind from one orange, using a channeling knife or potato peeler to produce long, thin strips with no pith. Squeeze the juice from both the oranges.

2. Put one third of the butter into a skillet and sauté the duck portions, skin side down, until they are crisp and brown. Turn several times until they are cooked through and have released most of their fat. Transfer to an ovenproof dish to keep warm.

3. Drain most of the fat from the pan in which the duck was cooked, leaving a tablespoon or so, and stir in the orange juice and stock. Cook briskly to reduce by half, then add the rum and ignite carefully using a long taper. Cook until the flames die down, then test for seasoning. Reduce the sauce a little more if necessary.

4. Add half the orange rind and cook for a few minutes more. To serve the duck, pour a little of the sauce over it and add a few more strips of orange rind. Serve accompanied by fresh vegetables.

DUCK AND RICE CASSEROLE (above right)
Duck is plentiful in Louisiana and, when crisply roasted, goes well with creamy rice.

Serves 4

INGREDIENTS:
4 duck leg portions
Salt and pepper
2 tbsp clear honey
1 tsp chopped fresh rosemary
1 tsp chopped fresh thyme
1¼ cups American long-grain rice
2½ cups chicken stock

the duck with the honey and herbs, return to the oven and cook for 8–10 minutes until golden brown.

6. Melt the butter in a pan, add the carrots and cook for 5 minutes, then add the mushrooms and cook for another 5 minutes, stirring occasionally.

7. Stir the carrots and mushrooms into the rice and adjust the seasoning to taste. Put the rice onto a serving dish and serve with the duck.

ROAST QUAIL WITH WILD RICE SAUTÉ (below)
Wild rice is in fact an aquatic grass which grows wild and is native to the Great Lakes region of North America, though it is now commercially cultivated. It has a nutty texture and flavor which is the perfect complement to game.

Serves 4

INGREDIENTS:
$1\frac{1}{4}$ cups wild rice
$2\frac{1}{3}$ cups water
Salt
4 slices of fat bacon
4 quails
$\frac{1}{2}$ cup butter
8 oz button mushrooms, sliced
1 bunch of scallions (green parts only), chopped

2 bay leaves
2 tbsp butter
2 carrots, finely chopped
6 oz chanterelle mushrooms, sliced

PREPARATION:
1. Preheat the oven to 400F.

2. Season the duck with the salt and pepper, prick the skin with a fork, then put the portions onto a rack in a roasting pan and cook for 15 minutes.

3. Mix together the honey and herbs and set aside.

4. Put the rice, stock, bay leaves and some salt into a heatproof casserole dish, slowly bring to a boil, cover with a lid, and cook in the oven for 30–40 minutes.

5. Increase the oven temperature to 425F. Lightly brush

PREPARATION:

1. Preheat the oven to 425F.

2. Put the rice, water and salt into a pan, bring to a boil, then simmer, covered, for 35–40 minutes until tender.

3. Wrap a slice of bacon around each quail, spread them with a little butter, put them into a pan, and roast for 25–30 minutes until cooked through. Remove the quail from the oven and leave to rest for 10 minutes.

4. Drain the rice and set it aside.

5. Melt a little more butter in a pan, add the mushrooms, and cook for 1 minute. Add the scallions and cook for a further 2 minutes.

6. Stir the rice into the pan and heat through. Spoon the rice mixture into a bowl and serve with the quail.

CAJUN SPICED LAMB WITH RICE (below left)
Fresh okra has a unique flavor all its own and gives a particularly smooth texture to a dish. However, canned okra can be used and is almost as good.

Serves 4

INGREDIENTS:
2 tbsp vegetable oil
1 lb 2 oz lean ground lamb
14 oz canned chopped tomatoes
Salt and pepper
1 tsp Cajun seasoning
14 oz canned okra, drained
Juice of 2 lemons
1 clove of garlic, crushed
1¼ cups American long-grain rice
2¼ cups lamb or chicken stock
1 lime, quartered
2 tbsp pine nuts

PREPARATION:

1. Heat 1 tablespoon of oil in a pan, add the lamb, and cook briskly until browned. Drain off the excess fat.

2. Stir in the tomatoes, salt and pepper and the Cajun seasoning. Bring to a boil, cover, and simmer for 15–20 minutes until the meat is cooked.

3. Add the okra and lemon juice and simmer, uncovered, for 10 minutes.

4. Meanwhile, heat the remaining oil in a pan, add the garlic, and cook for 1 minute, then stir in the rice and cook over a medium heat for 1 minute. Pour on the stock, bring to a boil, then simmer for 15 minutes until the rice is tender and the liquid has been absorbed.

5. Stir the lime quarters and pine nuts into the meat and cook for 2 minutes more. Put the rice into a serving dish, spoon the meat over it, and serve immediately.

BARBECUED COUNTRY RIBS WITH GLAZE
Pork ribs are especially delicious smothered in a rich glaze and barbecued slowly. Serve with coleslaw, potato salad and pinto beans.

Serves 4

INGREDIENTS:
1 cup cider vinegar
1/2 cup butter
2 tbsp lemon juice
3 tbsp Worcestershire sauce
3 tbsp cooking sherry
1 tsp salt
1/2 tsp hot pepper sauce
4 tbsp honey
1 tbsp soy sauce
3 lb ribs
2 tbsp mustard
4 tbsp light brown sugar

PREPARATION:
1. Place the vinegar, butter, lemon juice, Worcestershire sauce, sherry, salt, pepper sauce, honey and soy sauce into a saucepan. Heat, stirring until blended.

2. Season the ribs well and place them in this marinade, turning them a few times. Leave in the refrigerator for 2–3 hours or overnight, turning regularly.

3. When ready to cook, place the ribs on the barbecue, or broil or roast them in the oven. Cook them slowly, basting approximately every 15 minutes with the marinade.

4. While the meat is cooking, mix the mustard and brown sugar together. Spread the glaze all over the meat when it is nearly done.

5. Leave to cook for 10 minutes more on each side. Serve hot.

ALLIGATOR CREOLE (above right)
This is a serious stew, heavily spiced, thick and rich, and containing plenty of vegetables. Turkey, chicken or pork can be used as alternatives.

Serves 4

INGREDIENTS:
4–5 tbsp sunflower oil
1 large onion, sliced
2–3 cloves of garlic, peeled and finely chopped

1 large yellow or red pepper, seeded and sliced
4 medium tomatoes, peeled and quartered
1 lb alligator meat, cut into chunks and seasoned with pepper and salt
1–2 tsp cayenne
Salt and black pepper
1–2 tbsp tomato purée
1 cup chicken stock or water
Small glass of wine
Pinch of sugar
6 oz fine green beans, topped, tailed and halved
6 oz tiny sweetcorns
Sprigs of basil

PREPARATION:
1. Heat the oil in a large pan and sauté the onion until tender. Add the garlic, peppers, tomatoes and alligator meat and cook over a gentle heat for 2–3 minutes.

2. Add the seasonings, the tomato purée, the stock, wine and sugar, and cook gently for 20–30 minutes, stirring occasionally, until the meat is tender.

3. Meanwhile, blanch the beans and corn in boiling water for 2–3 minutes, then drain and add to the pot.

4. Serve the stew with a scattering of fresh basil leaves and a side dish of rice.

FISH ENTRÉES

SWINGIN' LOUISIANA GUMBO (below)

A gumbo lies somewhere between a thick soup and a thin stew. The name is thought to have originated in the French-based patois spoken by some African-Americans and Creoles in Louisiana. Okra is considered the essential ingredient, as it adds a rich and luscious quality to the stew. If fresh oysters are not available, use clams, scallops, or even mussels.

Serves 4–6

INGREDIENTS:
12 oysters in their shells
2 tbsp butter
2 medium onions, finely chopped
1½ tbsp flour

14 oz canned tomatoes
10 oz okra, cut into ½-inch pieces
5 cups fish stock
2 cloves of garlic, crushed
2 tsp salt
2 tsp Worcestershire sauce
1 tsp hot pepper sauce
1¼ cups American long-grain rice (optional)
1 lb large shrimp, peeled and deveined
8 oz fresh crabmeat

PREPARATION:
1. Carefully open the oysters, reserving their juice, and refrigerate them until required.

2. Melt the butter in a large heavy-based saucepan and cook the onions for 10 minutes over a low heat, stirring from time to time. Add the flour and cook for 2 minutes, stirring all the while.

3. Stir in the tomatoes and okra, bring to a boil, and cook for 5 minutes until the mixture thickens slightly.

4. Add the juice from the oysters and the fish stock to the okra pan. Stir in the garlic, salt, Worcestershire sauce and hot pepper sauce. Bring to a boil, cover with a lid, and cook over a low heat for 1 hour, stirring occasionally.

5. If using, cook the rice in boiling salted water for 12–15 minutes until tender. Drain and set aside.

6. Add the oysters, shrimp and crabmeat to the pan and cook for a further 5 minutes until the fish is tender.

7. Stir the cooked rice into the pan and heat through or serve separately as a side dish.

NEW ORLEANS FISH CREOLE (above right)

The white fish can be replaced by large shrimp, but reduce the cooking time accordingly, as shrimp must not be overcooked.

Serves 4

INGREDIENTS:
2 tbsp butter
1 large onion, chopped
1 garlic clove, crushed
2 sticks of celery, chopped

gently, covered, for 10–15 minutes until it is tender. Remove the fish and keep it warm.

3. Cook the sauce for a further 10 minutes until it has reduced and thickened.

4. Meanwhile, place the rice in the stock, bring to a boil, cover and simmer for 12–15 minutes until tender and the liquid has been absorbed.

5. Put the rice in a serving dish, pour over the sauce, arrange the fish on top, and serve garnished with the green pepper, orange slices and basil.

SHRIMP CREOLE (below)
For a spicier flavor, increase the Creole or Cajun seasoning, or add fresh chili according to taste.

14 oz canned chopped tomatoes
Salt and pepper
1 tsp curry powder
1 tsp Worcestershire sauce
½ tsp Tabasco sauce
8 fillets of sole, rolled and secured with cocktail sticks
1¼ cups American long-grain rice
2¼ cups fish stock

Garnish:
1 green pepper, seeded and thinly sliced
Orange slices
Fresh basil leaves

PREPARATION:
1. Heat the butter in a frying pan, add the onion, garlic and celery, and cook for 5–7 minutes until the vegetables soften. Stir in the tomatoes and all the seasonings, including the Worcestershire and Tabasco sauces, and bring to a boil.

2. Place the fish on top of the sauce and simmer

Serves 4

INGREDIENTS:
2 tbsp sunflower oil
1 large onion, chopped
2 cloves of garlic, crushed
1 tbsp Creole or Cajun seasoning, or Tabasco sauce
Salt
Small jar of tomato pasta sauce (Napolitana)
4 oz carrots, chopped
4 oz pumpkin or squash, chopped
$3/4$ cup fish or chicken stock
1 red pepper, seeded and sliced
3 oz zucchini, sliced
1 large firm banana, cut into 8 lengthways
6 oz large shrimp, peeled and deveined
Toasted flaked almonds

PREPARATION:
1. Heat the oil in a wok or large skillet and fry the onion and garlic for 2 minutes. Add the seasoning or Tabasco sauce, tomato sauce, carrots, pumpkin and stock, and cook over a medium heat for 10 minutes, stirring occasionally.

2. Add the pepper and zucchini and cook for 2 minutes. Stir in the banana and shrimp and cook for a further 2 minutes.

3. Serve with rice topped with toasted flaked almonds.

SHELLFISH ÉTOUFFÉE (opposite)
This is a quick and easy dish which, though slightly spiked with chili, is spicy rather than hot.

Serves 4

INGREDIENTS:
6 tbsp butter
2 large onions, finely chopped
1 tbsp flour
$1/2$ cup white wine or water
4 sticks of celery, chopped
1 red or green pepper, seeded and finely chopped
2 cloves of garlic, chopped
1 tsp cayenne
8 oz peeled crawfish or lobster tails
1 lb large shrimp, peeled and deveined
1 tbsp chopped parsley
Salt and black pepper

PREPARATION:
1. Melt the butter in a skillet or large frying pan and gently sauté the onion until tender. Stir in the flour to produce a thin paste, then add the wine, blending it in well as it comes to a boil.

2. Add the celery, red pepper and garlic and simmer gently for about 5 minutes until the vegetables are tender.

3. Add the cayenne and the shellfish and cook for 10–15 minutes, stirring frequently until they turn pink. Season to taste and serve with rice.

FRIED SOFTSHELL CRAB WITH OYSTER DRESSING
This Louisiana specialty is a treat rarely found elsewhere. Several times a year the Blue crab sheds its hard shell and, if caught immediately before the next shell begins to develop, is edible in its entirety. Strange as this may seem, it is quite delicious deep- or pan-fried and served hot with a rice dressing.

Serves 4

INGREDIENTS:
8–10 small oysters in their shells
6 tbsp butter
1 large onion, chopped
3 sticks of celery, chopped
$1/2$ green pepper, finely chopped
$1/4$ tsp each salt, paprika, cayenne, black pepper, onion powder, dried oregano, and thyme
2 cloves of garlic, crushed
1–2 bay leaves
$1/2$ cup rice
4 oz shrimp, peeled, deveined and roughly chopped
3 tbsp heavy cream
2 tbsp chopped scallions

Fried crab:
4 cleaned and prepared softshell crabs (see below)
$1/2$ cup all-purpose flour
$1/2$ cup fine cornmeal
Salt and pepper
Oil for deep-frying
Lemons to garnish

PREPARATION:
1. Shuck the oysters and place them in a bowl with their juice and $3/4$ cup water. Refrigerate until required.

2. Melt the butter in a heavy-based pan and add the onion, celery, pepper, seasonings, garlic and bay leaves. Stir over a high heat for 1 minute to soften slightly, then add the rice.

3. Stir the rice well to coat it, then add ¾ cup water. Cook gently for about 5 minutes until the water has become absorbed, then stir in the oyster juice and water from which the oysters have been strained. Cook slowly for a further 5–7 minutes, stirring occasionally.

4. When the rice is almost cooked, stir in the shrimp, the cream and the oysters and cook for only 1–2 minutes. Then stir in the scallions and keep warm while you fry the crabs.

5. To prepare the crabs, wipe them clean and dry them. Mix the flour and cornmeal with plenty of the seasoning and dust the crabs thoroughly with this mixture.

6. Heat the oil in a deep-fryer to 320F. Add the crabs, one or two at a time, turning them so that they become evenly browned. Remove with a slotted spoon, drain on paper towels, and keep warm while you cook the others.

7. Serve as soon as possible with the rice and halves of lemon to squeeze over.

Tip: If the crabs have not already been prepared, this is what you do. With a pair of scissors, cut the front part away, including the eyes and mouth, then pull back each side of the top shell and carefully remove the greyish "dead men's fingers" (gills). Then turn the crab over and pull off the tail flap or "apron."

CRAB CLAWS WITH PLUM DIP (right)
During the crab season (April to October), the Blue crab is so readily available around New Orleans that it finds its way into almost everything, from luxurious appetizers to the ever-popular street snack.

Serves 4
INGREDIENTS:
12 large cooked crab legs

Sauce:
6 tbsp hoisin sauce
2 tbsp plum sauce

Garnish:
A few thin julienne strips of fresh ginger
Cilantro leaves (optional)

PREPARATION:
1. Mix together the hoisin and plum sauces and spoon into small dishes to serve with the crab claws.

2. Alternatively, the meat could be removed beforehand. Crack the lower part of the crab leg, near to the claw end, and gently twist away the claw, revealing the core of white meat.

3. Scrape the meat from inside the claw and leg with a small skewer and repeat with the remaing claws. Divide the crabmeat between four serving plates, sprinkle with the ginger, and garnish with cilantro leaves.

CRAB AND POTATO FRIES (right)
For occasions when finger foods are appropriate, these firm favorites can be threaded onto wooden skewers for serving, perhaps interspersed with small bay leaves to add a touch of color and flavor.

Serves 4

INGREDIENTS:
1 lb sweet potatoes or yams, sliced into ½-inch slices
8 oz floury potatoes, cut small
Salt and pepper
6 tbsp unsalted butter
6 scallions, chopped
2 cloves of garlic, crushed
1-inch piece of fresh ginger, finely chopped
½ tsp chili powder
12 oz white crabmeat, flaked
1 egg, beaten
2 cups dried breadcrumbs
Oil for deep frying

Sauce:
6 tbsp mango chutney
6 tbsp vegetable stock
½ tsp ground allspice
½ tsp turmeric

PREPARATION:
1. Place the sweet potatoes or yams into a pan of salted water, bring to a boil, and cook for 5 minutes, then add the potatoes and cook for a further 12–15 minutes until tender. Drain thoroughly, then mash until smooth, adding seasoning and beating in 4 tablespoons of butter.

2. Melt the remaining butter in a small pan, add the scallions, garlic, ginger and chili. Cook until the vegetables are soft (2–3 minutes), then fold into the potatoes. Spread this mixture over a plate, leave it to cool, then refrigerate for ½ hour.

3. Stir the crabmeat into the potato mixture, then divide and roll the mixture into 20 even-sized croquettes.

4. Brush the croquettes with the beaten egg and coat them well with the breadcrumbs. Place in the refrigerator for a further ½ hour to thoroughly chill.

5. Meanwhile, put all the sauce ingredients into a pan and simmer for 5–10 minutes until the mixture has reduced and thickened.

6. Heat the oil in a deep-fryer to 350F, testing the heat with a cube of bread, which should brown almost immediately. Fry 5–6 croquettes at a time for 3–4 minutes until golden brown. Drain on kitchen paper and keep warm. Repeat the process with the remainder.

7. Serve immediately, accompanied by the sauce.

SHRIMP IN BEER BATTER WITH ONION MARMALADE
Shrimp or crawfish can both be cooked in this deliciously light and tasty batter which should be prepared in advance and left in the refrigerator until rested and slightly chilled.

Serves 4

INGREDIENTS:
1 tsp cayenne
$\frac{1}{2}$ tsp each salt, paprika, black pepper, garlic powder or flakes, onion powder
$\frac{3}{4}$ cup all-purpose flour
1 egg
3 tbsp beer
2 tbsp coconut milk
1 tsp baking soda
24 medium-sized shrimp, shelled and deveined
Oil for deep-frying

Onion marmalade:
2 onions, chopped
2 tbsp dark-brown sugar
4 tbsp orange marmalade
1 tsp Tabasco or hot pepper sauce
1 tbsp sherry or red wine vinegar
1 tbsp tomato ketchup

PREPARATION:
1. Thoroughly mix the first 6 seasonings together. In a separate bowl mix $\frac{1}{2}$ cup flour with 1 teaspoon of the seasoning.

2. Beat the egg, then beat in the rest of the flour, another teaspoon of seasoning mix, the beer, coconut milk and the baking soda.

3. Heat the oil in a deep-fryer to 350F.

4. Sprinkle the shrimp with seasoned flour and shake off the excess. Dip them into the batter, allowing any excess to drip off before carefully dropping them into the hot fat. Cook in batches of 7 or 8 for only about $\frac{1}{2}$ minute until crisp and golden and cooked through.

5. Drain on paper towels and keep warm while cooking the rest.

6. In a non-stick pan, heat all the ingredients for the Onion Marmalade together until the sugar has dissolved. Cook gently until the onions have softened and the sauce thickened. Use immediately with the Shrimp in Beer Batter or cool and store for up to 3 weeks in a refrigerator.

SEAFOOD CRÊPES (right)
Make the batter in advance and leave it to chill and rest in the refrigerator. It is even possible to make the crêpes on the previous day.

Makes 8

INGREDIENTS:
Crêpes:
2 eggs
1 cup all-purpose flour
A pinch of salt
1 cup milk
1 tbsp oil or melted butter
Extra oil for frying

Filling:
4 tbsp butter
1 onion, finely chopped
2 sticks of celery, finely chopped
2 scallions, trimmed and chopped
1 tbsp flour
1 cup heavy cream
1 lb peeled crawfish tails or shrimp
8 oz white crabmeat
A squeeze of lemon juice
Pinch of cayenne
Sprigs of tarragon or parsley to garnish

PREPARATION:
1. Beat the eggs in a large bowl, add the flour and salt and continue beating to a thick paste. Then whisk in the milk and oil or butter with electric beaters or a hand whisk to produce a smooth batter. Chill, covered, for 30 minutes.

2. Lightly grease a heavy-based non-stick 8-inch skillet and heat it until a light haze appears. Pour in 2–3 tablespoons of batter, enough to cover the base of the pan, and swirl it around to give a thin coating.

3. Cook until the crêpe comes loose from the pan and is just golden underneath. Turn over or toss and cook

for 1–2 minutes on the other side until set and golden. Slide out onto paper towels and leave to cool while cooking the rest.

4. Stack the pancakes between wax paper and chill or store until required.

5. In a medium pan, heat the butter and cook the onion, celery and scallions until tender. Sprinkle on the flour and stir to a thick paste.

6. Gradually stir in the cream and bring to a gentle boil, stirring all the time. Boil for 1–2 minutes until the sauce thickens, then add the crawfish and crabmeat and bring back to a gentle bubble, stirring frequently.

7. Add the lemon juice and cayenne to taste, then cool slightly before filling and folding the pancakes. Add a sprig of tarragon or parsley before serving.

PIQUANT SEAFOOD BITES (overleaf)
Monkfish is perhaps the best choice for this dish as it is a firm fish which keeps its shape and texture during cooking; but any firm white fish would do.

Serves 4

INGREDIENTS:
10 oz firm white fish, skinned and boned
6 oz large shrimp, peeled and deveined
1 cup all-purpose flour
1 tsp easy-blend dried yeast
Salt and pepper
Finely grated rind of 1 lemon
3/4 cup beer
Oil for deep frying

Garnish:
Cilantro leaves
Lemon wedges

47

PREPARATION:

1. Cut the fish and shrimp into small pieces.

2. Sift the flour into a bowl. Stir in the yeast, seasoning and lemon rind, and gradually beat in the beer to form a smooth batter. Leave to stand for 15 minutes.

3. Heat the oil in a deep-fryer to 350F. Dip the fish pieces in the batter and fry for 3–4 minutes until golden brown. Use a slotted spoon to lift them from the pan, then drain them on paper towels.

4. Serve immediately garnished with the cilantro and lemon wedges.

Tip: Serve with mayonnaise or a spicy salsa.

BLACKENED FISH STEAKS (above)

This is a fast and fierce way of cooking firm fish. It was made so popular by Paul Prudhomme during the 1980s that it has become one of the classics of Creole cooking. The fish should be only slightly charred on the outside but still succulent in the middle. It should not resemble burnt toast!

Serves 3

INGREDIENTS:
2 tsp paprika
1$^{1}/_{2}$ tsp salt
$^{1}/_{2}$ tsp each onion powder, garlic powder, white pepper, black pepper, dried dill and dried oregano
3 thick fish steaks, e.g. catfish, cod, salmon, shark,

swordfish or tuna
6 tbsp butter
Lemon wedges to garnish

PREPARATION:
1. Mix all 8 seasonings together, then dip the fish steaks into the mixture to coat them well.

2. Heat half the butter in a large frying pan until it is on the point of turning brown. Add the steaks and cook them on each side, taking their thickness into account, until they are only just cooked through.

3. Transfer them immediately to an ovenproof dish and keep warm. Add the rest of the butter to the pan and heat it until it sizzles, then spoon the seasoned butter quickly over the fish. Serve with lemon wedges and plenty of fresh bread.

FRIED FISH FILLETS WITH SHRIMP SAUCE (below left)
Any fillets of firm white fish can be cooked in this highly seasoned breadcrumb coating. The most traditional and most widely available is catfish, but other fish such as trout, snapper or flounder are also suitable.

Serves 4

INGREDIENTS:
Fish fillets:
1 cup flour
3 tbsp fine dried breadcrumbs
1 tsp salt
1 tsp cayenne
1 tsp paprika
1 tsp garlic powder
1 tsp white pepper
$1/2$ tsp onion powder
1 egg
Milk
4 large or 8 small fish fillets
Oil for frying

Shrimp sauce:
2 tbsp butter
1 small onion, finely chopped
1 tbsp flour
$1/2$ cup stock or milk
Salt
$1/2$ tsp each cayenne, black, and white pepper
3–4 tbsp heavy cream
2 oz button mushrooms, sliced
2 oz small cooked shrimp, shelled

PREPARATION:
1. Sift half the flour, together with all the dry ingredients for the fish fillets, onto a large shallow plate. Break the egg into a small bowl, beat it with 2–3 tablespoons of milk and pour this into another large shallow plate. Sift the remaining flour onto a third plate.

2. Dip the fish first into the flour, then the egg, and then into the seasonings mixture. Shake off the excess and set aside.

3. Heat at least 2 inches of oil in a deep frying pan until a slight haze appears on the surface. Carefully put 2 or 3 pieces of fish in at a time and cook for 2 minutes on each side until crisp and golden.

4. Remove with a slotted spoon and drain on paper towels. Keep warm while you cook the rest.

5. To prepare the sauce, heat the butter in a small pan and fry the onion until tender. Sprinkle on the flour, stir to a paste, and cook for one minute.

6. Blend in the stock and stir frequently as it comes to a boil to prevent any lumps from forming. Cook for another minute or two, stirring well, and when smooth and thick stir in the seasonings, cream, mushrooms and shrimp.

7. Cook gently for a further 3–4 minutes until the mushrooms are cooked. Check the seasoning before serving with the fish.

SOLE FILLETS IN HOT TOMATO SAUCE (below)
Tomatoes go very well with fish, but the addition of orange juice and Tabasco brings an intriguing piquancy to the dish.

Serves 4

INGREDIENTS:
3 tbsp sunflower or vegetable oil

1 large onion, sliced
2 sticks of celery, chopped
14 oz canned chopped tomatoes
1 tbsp Tabasco or hot chili sauce
Juice of 1 large fresh orange
1 yellow or orange pepper, seeded and sliced
Salt and black pepper
8 small fillets of sole, flounder, trout or catfish
Sprigs of flat-leaf parsley

PREPARATION:
1. Heat the oil in a medium-sized pan and sauté the onion until translucent. Add the celery, tomatoes, Tabasco sauce and orange juice and simmer gently for about 15 minutes or until the sauce has slightly reduced and the flavors have melded. Add the peppers and cook for a further 2–3 minutes. Season well.

2. Spoon the sauce into a large skillet and arrange the fish on top. Simmer gently for about 5 minutes until the fish appears very lightly cooked.

3. Serve with rice, or rice and peas or beans, decorated with a few sprigs of parsley.

CORN-CRUSTED COD FILLETS WITH SALSA (below left)
Fine cornmeal makes a crisp and tasty coating for any fish fillets. Salsa, a modern culinary term for a finely diced, chilled salad or uncooked relish, provides a lively contrast to the hot delicate fish.

Serves 4

INGREDIENTS:
Fillets:
1 tbsp cornstarch
$\frac{1}{2}$ cup fine cornmeal
Salt and white pepper
4 large or 8 small fillets of cod
$\frac{1}{2}$ cup butter

Salsa:
$\frac{1}{2}$ each small red and yellow peppers
$\frac{1}{2}$ red chili, seeded and finely chopped
1 small red onion, finely chopped
2 medium firm red tomatoes, seeded and finely chopped
2-inch piece of cucumber, peeled and cut into small dice
1 clove of garlic, very thinly sliced
$\frac{3}{4}$ cup olive oil
1 tbsp chopped mint
Juice of $\frac{1}{2}$ a large lemon

PREPARATION:
1. Mix together the cornstarch, cornmeal and seasonings. Dip each fillet in this mixture and coat thoroughly.

2. Heat some of the butter and cook the fillets, a few at a time, for 2–3 minutes on each side until crisp and golden. Drain on paper towels.

3. Mix together all the chopped and prepared ingredients for th salsa. Add the oil, mint, and lemon juice and season to taste.

SPAGHETTI WITH CLAMS (right)
This delicious dish, known in Italy as spaghetti con vongole*, can be prepared with other shellfish such as mussels. Serve it accompanied by a green salad.*

Serves 4

INGREDIENTS:
1 lb spaghetti

Salt
3¼ lb baby clams
4 tbsp olive oil
2 cloves of garlic, crushed
1 small onion, sliced
1 glass of dry white wine
14 oz canned chopped tomatoes
1 tsp chopped red chili
1 tbsp fresh chopped parsley

PREPARATION:

1. Cook the spaghetti in boiling salted water for 10–12 minutes or *al dente.*

2. Wash the clams in salted water, rinse them well and dry them thoroughly.

3. Heat 2 tablespoons of oil in a large pan, add the clams and garlic, cover with a tightly fitting lid, and cook over a gentle heat for 5–6 minutes until the clams open. Discard any that do not open.

4. Heat the remaining oil in another pan, fry the onion for 3–4 minutes until tender, add the wine, tomatoes and chili. Add the clams to this mixture. Bring to a boil and simmer for 5–6 minutes.

5. Drain the spaghetti, place it in a warmed serving dish and pour over the sauce. Serve immediately, sprinkled with parsley.

CRAWFISH BOIL (left)

This is an occasion, a celebration, an extravagance! Traditionally, a mountain of crawfish or other shellfish, enough for a crowd, is cooked by the men rather than the women, much like the traditional barbecue. Use your fingers to deal with these succulent morsels, pulling them apart and sucking the sweet flesh from their shells.

Serves 4–6

INGREDIENTS:
Seasoning mix (2 oz paprika, 1 oz each celery salt and
  mustard powder, 1 tsp ground allspice, ½ tsp whole
  cloves, a few bay leaves)
2 large onions, quartered
1 whole head of garlic, unpeeled and crushed
2 lemons, cut into wedges
4 small red-skinned potatoes, unpeeled and halved

1 tbsp cayenne – more if required
Small bunch of fresh cilantro, chopped
1 large green pepper, seeded and quartered
2 ears of corn, cut into 3 or 4 pieces
6–7 lb uncooked crawfish, large shrimp, crab or other
  shellfish

PREPARATION:

1. Mix the seasoning ingredients together and place in a very large pan with 2½ cups water. Blend well, then add the onion, garlic, lemons, potatoes, cayenne, and another 5 quarts of water.

2. Bring to a boil, then simmer for 15–20 minutes.

3. Add the cilantro, green pepper, corn and shellfish, stir well, then bring back to a boil. Simmer for a further 5 minutes, then turn off the heat and leave to stand for at least 10 minutes before serving.

4. Provide each guest with a large soup bowl filled with crawfish. Let them come back for a helping of the broth if they have any room left!

VEGETABLES & SIDES

PECAN AND RAISIN CORN DRESSING (below)

A dressing, apart from being something you put on your salad, can also be a stuffing or side dish, usually served with meat or fish. This one contains pecans which, when roasted, develop a warm and lively flavor that is excellent with poultry and roasts.

Serves 5-6

INGREDIENTS:
1 cup pecans
2 tbsp vegetable or sunflower oil
1 large onion, finely chopped
1 green pepper, seeded and finely chopped
1 tsp salt
$\frac{1}{2}$ tsp white pepper
2 tsp prepared mustard
1 tsp paprika
1 tsp black pepper
$1\frac{1}{2}$ cups stale cornbread, finely crumbled
$\frac{1}{2}$ cup raisins, chopped
$\frac{3}{4}$ cup rich brown meat stock
2 tbsp melted butter

PREPARATION:
1. Spread the nuts out on a cookie sheet and roast them at 350F for about 10 minutes until crisp and dark brown. Cool, then roughly chop or crush.

2. Heat the oil in a medium pan and fry the onion until translucent. Add the green pepper, salt and seasonings and cook for 2–3 minutes, stirring all the while.

3. Mix in the nuts, cornbread crumbs and raisins until evenly blended. Gradually stir in sufficient stock to bring the dressing together and give a spoonable consistency. Finally, stir in the butter. Use as a stuffing or spoon into an ovenproof dish and bake at 350F for 20 minutes, covered, and serve as a side dish.

SWEET POTATO BAKE (right)

Sweet potatoes and yams are so similar that either could be used in this recipe, as could members of the pumpkin and squash family. Use whatever is available.

Serves 6

INGREDIENTS:
2 leeks, trimmed
2 lb sweet potatoes or yams, peeled and sliced
2 tbsp butter
3 large eggs
$1\frac{1}{4}$ cups milk
4 tbsp heavy cream
2 cloves of garlic, crushed
Salt and black pepper
1 tsp paprika
$\frac{1}{2}$ tsp grated nutmeg
Chopped scallions

PREPARATION:
1. Wash the leeks thoroughly and slice them. Layer the potatoes and leeks in a well-buttered ovenproof dish. Heat the oven to 350F.

2. Beat together the eggs, milk, cream, garlic and seasonings. Pour evenly over the sweet potatoes and dot with butter. Sprinle with paprika and nutmeg and scatter with the scallions.

3. Bake for about one hour, or until the potatoes are tender and the top golden. (Check occasionally to make sure they are not becoming too brown, in which case the dish can be covered with aluminum foil.)

APRICOT RICE WITH ROASTED SQUASH (right)
This is a delicious and economical vegetarian supper combination which could also be served with boiled ham, chicken or sausages, if you wish.

Serves 4

INGREDIENTS:
1 lb butternut or acorn squash
6 tbsp butter
1 tbsp light brown sugar
Salt
1 large onion, finely chopped
2 cloves of garlic, crushed
2 sticks of celery, finely chopped
1 cup leftover rice
¾ cup vegetable stock
4 oz dried ready-to-eat apricots
2 oz raisins
1 tsp black pepper
1 tbsp Worcestershire sauce
Fresh parsley

PREPARATION:
1. Peel and dice the squash. Preheat the oven to 400F.

2. Melt 4 tbsp of the butter in a pan with the sugar and a pinch of salt and toss the squash in this. Transfer to an ovenproof dish and cook in the oven for about 30 minutes, stirring and turning the squash occasionally.

3. Heat the rest of the butter in a medium pan and fry the onion, garlic and celery until translucent. Add the rice, the stock, the dried fruit and seasonings, and stir over a high heat for 5–6 minutes until the stock is absorbed and the rice is thoroughly heated through.

4. Keep the rice warm until the squash is ready and serve them together, garnished with parsley.

STUFFED PUMPKIN OR SQUASH
In the fall, when pumpkins are abundant, this is a delicious way to serve them for a good, economical family meal.

Serves 4–6

INGREDIENTS:
2 tbsp olive or sunflower oil
1 medium onion, finely chopped
2 cloves of garlic, finely chopped
4 medium tomatoes, skinned, seeded and diced
1 green or red pepper, seeded and chopped
1 lb ground beef or lamb
$1\frac{1}{4}$ cups beef or lamb stock
$\frac{1}{2}$ cup American long-grain rice
1 small pumpkin or 2 small squashes (butternut or acorn)
Salt and freshly ground black pepper
1 tbsp Tabasco sauce
1 tbsp mustard
1 tbsp finely chopped parsley
1 tsp finely chopped basil

PREPARATION:
1. Heat 1 tablespoon of oil in a large pan, add the onion and garlic, and fry gently for two minutes until translucent. Add the tomatoes and peppers and cook for another 3–4 minutes.

2. Add the meat and fry until browned all over, then reduce the heat and cook very gently for 5–10 minutes.

3. In another pan, heat the stock to boiling point, then pour in the rice, cover, and cook for about 10 minutes, checking occasionally to make sure it doesn't dry out.

4. If you have one pumpkin, cut it in half lengthways and scoop out the seeds. If you have smaller squashes, cut them in half according to their shape and remove the seeds. Cut slices from the bases so that they stand steadily, and season with salt and pepper. Place in an ovenproof dish. Preheat the oven to 375F.

5. Remove the pan of meat from the heat. When the rice is nearly tender and all the liquid absorbed, add to the meat and mix in well.

6. Add the Tabasco sauce, mustard, parsley, basil and seasoning to taste. Then spoon into the center of the pumpkin or squashes and cover with aluminum foil. Bake for 30–50 minutes according to the size and thickness of their flesh.

Tip: You could prepare this dish in advance, ready to reheat in a microwave for 4–5 minutes, covered.

CHILIED TOMATO AND PEPPER CHUTNEY (right)
This is delicious with cold cuts, cornbreads and rice dressings. It is hot though, so you can reduce the chili if you wish.

Makes 5 lb

INGREDIENTS:
$6\frac{1}{2}$ lb tomatoes
3 onions
6 cloves of garlic, peeled and chopped
1 red and 1 yellow pepper, seeded and sliced
2 red or green chilies, seeded and chopped
1 tsp cayenne
1 tbsp mustard seeds
1 tbsp coriander seeds
1 tbsp turmeric powder
1 cup light brown sugar
$1\frac{1}{4}$ cups white wine vinegar

PREPARATION:
1. Cut a cross on the top of each tomato. Place in a large bowl and pour boiling water over them. Leave for 5 minutes, drain, then peel away the skins and dice the flesh.

2. Peel and finely chop the onions and place them in a large preserving pan with the chopped tomatoes, garlic, peppers and chili. Stir in the cayenne, mustard seeds, coriander seeds, turmeric, sugar and vinegar. Bring to a boil over a medium heat, stirring constantly.

3. Reduce the heat and simmer until the chutney begins to thicken (about 1 hour); however, this may take longer if the tomatoes are very watery.

4. Ladle into clean, warmed jars, then cool and refrigerate for up to one month.

HOT PEPPER SALSA (overleaf left)
This is a quick-to-cook Tex-Mex-style relish which you can make as hot or as mild as you like by increasing or decreasing the amount of chili used. It is delicious with barbecued and chargrilled meats, spicy sausages, fish or vegetables, and many well-seasoned cold dishes.

Makes $1\frac{1}{2}$ lb

INGREDIENTS:
1 red onion, finely chopped

6 tbsp white wine vinegar
8 tbsp sugar
Juice and finely grated rind of 1 large orange
1 red pepper, seeded and chopped
1 orange pepper, seeded and chopped
½ small red chili, seeded and chopped
4 tomatoes, peeled and chopped
10–12 ready-to-eat dried apricots, chopped

PREPARATION:
1. Put the onion, vinegar and sugar into a large pan, bring to a boil, then continue boiling until the sugar has dissolved.

2. Add the orange juice and the rind, the peppers and chili, and cook for 8–10 minutes until most of the liquid has evaporated.

3. Stir in the tomatoes and apricots and cook gently for 5 minutes. Pack into warm clean jars and chill for 1–2

days before using. Store in the refrigerator, but only for 2–3 weeks.

APPLE AND CRANBERRY JELLY (above)
Sharp, yet sweet and fruity, this ruby jelly is great with so many meats and cooked dishes, yet is also delicious in crêpes and with ice cream.

Makes about 4½ lb

INGREDIENTS:
4 lb apples, wiped, quartered and cored
1 lb 2 oz cranberries
1 cinnamon stick
Sugar

PREPARATION:
1. Place the apples in a large pan with the cinnamon stick and the cranberries. Just cover with water, bring to a boil, then simmer until soft (about 40 minutes).

60

2. Soak a jelly bag in water and wring it out, then hang it up over a very large bowl. Pour in all the fruits and juices and leave, untouched, until all the liquid has drained out. If you try to speed things up by pushing the juice through, the resulting liquid will not be perfectly clear.

3. Measure the juice and allow 8 oz sugar for every cup of juice. Place juice and sugar into a large enamel or stainless steel pan. Bring to a boil slowly so that the sugar can dissolve and then simmer, uncovered, spooning off any scum that rises to the surface.

4. Boil gently until setting point is reached (220F). To test, place a small plate briefly in the freezer, then drop a spoonful of the jelly onto the plate and leave it to cool. The jelly is ready if it forms a skin that wrinkles when you push your finger through it. If not, continue boiling for a further few minutes, but do test frequently.

5. Pack into clean warm jars, cool, refrigerate and use within one month.

COLLARD GREENS AND BACON
Ideally, pickled pork would be more authentic, but fat bacon, bought in a piece and cut into lardons, works just as well. Young cabbage or turnip or mustard greens can also be substituted.

Serves 4

INGREDIENTS:
2 lb greens
1/2 lb bacon, cut into lardons
1 large onion, finely chopped
1 small dried chili, seeds removed and finely chopped (optional)
1/2 tsp sugar
Salt and freshly ground black pepper

PREPARATION:
1. Wash the greens very thoroughly and remove the tough stalks and veins. Stack the leaves together, a few at a time, roll them up, then cut into narrow ribbons.

2. Using a heavy-based skillet, gently cook the bacon pieces until the fat runs out and the meat has slightly browned. Add the onions and cook them until translucent, but do not brown them.

3. Shake the greens so that only a little water still adheres to the leaves, then add to the bacon and onions with the fat in the pan.

4. Add the rest of the ingredients, stir well, cover, and cook over a low heat until the greens are tender.

RED BEANS 'N' RICE
A typical Cajun Monday dish, this is economical, delicious and traditionally served with cornbread. For a meatier and spicier variation, see Beans and Rice Creole-Style (below).

Serves 4–6

INGREDIENTS:
1 lb dried red kidney beans, soaked overnight
1 ham hock, soaked overnight
2 tbsp vegetable oil
1 large onion, chopped
2 sticks of celery, chopped
1 green pepper, seeded and chopped
3 cloves of garlic, crushed
2 bay leaves
1 1/4 cups American long-grain rice
1/2 tsp each cayenne and black and white pepper
Salt (if necessary)

PREPARATION:
1. Wash the ham in cold water. Put it into a large pan, cover with water, bring to a boil, then cover with a lid and simmer for 1–1 1/2 hours until tender. Reserve the cooking liquid and make this up to 3 cups with water.

2. Meanwhile, rinse the beans under cold water and put them into a large pan with 7 cups of water. Bring to a boil, cover, and simmer for 1 hour until the beans are tender.

3. Heat the oil in a pan and fry the onion, celery, green pepper and garlic for 5 minutes, stirring occasionally. Add the bay leaves and cook for a further 5 minutes.

4. Stir in the rice and reserved ham stock, bring to a boil, then simmer for 15 minutes until the rice is tender and the liquid has been absorbed. Add the cayenne and the black and white peppers and salt.

5. Drain the beans and mash them until creamy. Slice the meat from the ham hock and add it to the beans.

Fluff up the rice and remove the bay leaves, then serve the beans over the rice or mix them together.

BEANS AND RICE CREOLE-STYLE (below)

Another of the many variations on the theme of beans and rice popular in this land of rice. Serve with warm cornbread.

Serves 4–6

INGREDIENTS:
$^3/_4$ cup dried red kidney beans, soaked overnight
$^3/_4$ cup dried white kidney beans, soaked overnight
12 oz hot spicy sausage (e.g. tasso or chorizo), sliced
1 large onion, chopped
1 clove of garlic, crushed
$1^1/_4$ cups chicken stock
$^1/_2$ tsp dried marjoram
1 bay leaf
$1^3/_4$ lb canned chopped tomatoes
$1^1/_4$ cups American long-grain rice
2 sticks of celery, chopped
1 red pepper, seeded and chopped
Salt and pepper

PREPARATION:
1. Rinse the beans under cold water, drain them, then place in a large pan with enough water to cover. Bring to a boil, cover with a lid, and simmer for $1^1/_4$–$1^1/_2$ hours until tender. Drain and set aside.

2. In a large pan, gently brown the sausage in its own fat. Add the onion and garlic and cook for 5 minutes until soft.

3. Add the beans, stock, marjoram, bay leaf, tomatoes and rice. Bring to a boil, cover, and simmer for 10 minutes, stirring occasionally.

4. Add the celery and red pepper and cook for a further 10–12 minutes until tender. Season well.

Tip: To save time, use canned beans; but rinse them well before use and be careful not to overcook them.

DIRTY RICE (right)

This is also called a rice dressing. It is not unlike a stuffing mixture and is often used for this purpose as well as for an economical family meal.

Serves 4

INGREDIENTS:
2 tbsp oil
1 onion, chopped
2 sticks of celery, chopped
1 small green pepper, seeded and chopped
2 cloves of garlic, crushed
8 oz chicken livers, very finely chopped
1 tsp cayenne
1 tsp cumin powder
½ tsp dried thyme
½ tsp black pepper
½ tsp salt
1¼ cups American long-grain rice
2¼ cups chicken stock

PREPARATION:
1. Heat the oil in a large saucepan and fry the onion, celery, green pepper and garlic for 5 minutes. Add the chicken livers, turning them until brown all over.

2. Stir in the seasonings and the rice. Cook for 1 minute. Stir in the chicken stock, bring to a boil, cover, then simmer for 12 minutes or until the rice is tender and the liquid has been absorbed.

MAQUECHOUX

Pronounced "mockshoe," this is a Cajun word that describes a dish containing corn. Every family has its own version: some eat it simply with rice and gravy, others add chicken, shrimp or crawfish. To enhance the corn's natural sweetness you can add extra sugar,

which makes it all the more delicious if you are serving it with spicy sausages or barbecued meats.

Serves 4–5

INGREDIENTS:
4 cups frozen or canned sweetcorn
2–3 tbsp butter
1 large onion, chopped
1 red and 1 green pepper, seeded and chopped
2 large tomatoes, seeded and chopped
Salt and black pepper
2 eggs, beaten

PREPARATION:
1. Place the corn in a food processor and blend it very briefly until it is reduced to a porridge-like consistency.

2. Heat the butter in a large pan or skillet and cook the onion and peppers until soft. Add the tomatoes and corn and cook for a further 5 minutes.

3. Season well, and just before serving, whisk in the eggs and allow them to lightly scramble in the heat of the mixture. Serve very hot.

Tip: If you wish to use fresh corn, cook about 8 trimmed cobs, then scrape off the kernels with a sharp knife and add as above. Allow extra cooking time when added to the other vegetables to make sure it is completely tender.

Cornbread

This is a staple served with many a simple dish. It can be made more savory by adding a handful of grated Parmesan cheese and extra seasoning, or sweet by adding sugar. Serve warm with melted butter for breakfast or with soups, or serve as the Italians do polenta, with a casserole of game or wild mushrooms.

Serves 6–8

INGREDIENTS:
2 cups white or yellow cornmeal or polenta
1 cup all-purpose flour
1 tsp salt
2 tsp baking powder
2 large or 3 medium eggs, beaten together
6 tbsp butter, melted
1 cup milk

PREPARATION:
1. Lightly grease and line a shallow baking pan measuring approximately 9 x 11 inches. Preheat the oven to 375F.

2. In a large mixing bowl, combine all the dry ingredients. Make a hollow in the center, then gradually work in the eggs, melted butter and milk, beating well to produce a smooth batter.

3. Pour into the prepared pan and bake for about 20 minutes or until just firm. Remove from the oven and cool slightly before serving with butter or as you prefer.

Tip: To serve as a dessert, add 6 tablespoons of sugar to the other dry ingredients and serve warm topped with maple syrup, or cooked berries and heavy cream or ice cream.

Pickled Okra

Okra plays an integral part in the cuisine of the American South. It is an unusually-shaped green vegetable, almost finger-like, which, with prolonged cooking, produces a sticky starchiness which helps to thicken gumbos. Crisply cooked, however, it is quite different. It is excellent breaded, deep-fried, or pickled as a substitute for dill pickles.

Makes about 3 lb

INGREDIENTS:
4 cups white wine or cider vinegar
$^3/_4$ cup water
4 oz salt
3–4 large cloves of garlic, peeled
Fresh red chilies
3 lb okra, washed and trimmed

PREPARATION:
1. Place the vinegar, water and salt in an enamel pan. Bring to a boil and add the okra. Bring back to a boil for 1 minute.

2. Pack into clean, hot jars, adding a clove of garlic and a chili to each jar. Cool, then store in the refrigerator. Use within three weeks.

Potato Salad (right)

In Louisiana, mashed hard-boiled egg yolks are sometimes added to this popular American side dish.

Serves 6

INGREDIENTS:
2 lb small new potatoes, scrubbed
1 small red onion, very finely chopped
1 stick of celery, chopped
$^1/_4$ cup fresh chopped parsley
1 cup good mayonnaise
2 tbsp red wine vinegar
Salt and freshly ground black pepper
4 chopped scallions
Chopped chives

PREPARATION:
1. Boil the potatoes whole and when cool enough to handle remove their skins. If small, leave them whole, or cut them into smaller pieces. (If using new potatoes the skins can be left on.)

2. In a large bowl, mix together the onion, celery, parsley, scallions, mayonnaise and vinegar, then add the potatoes. Add salt and pepper and combine everything together thoroughly.

3. Garnish with a scattering of chopped chives.

DESSERTS

BEIGNETS WITH RASPBERRY AND APRICOT SAUCES
(below)
These mouthfuls of sweet batter are deep-fried until delicately crisp, then served with two tangy fruit sauces. Eat them while they are still hot and as light as a feather.

Serves 4

INGREDIENTS:
8 oz raspberries
4 tbsp superfine sugar
Small can of apricots in juice
1 tbsp rum
9 level tbsp all-purpose flour
Pinch of salt
4 tbsp butter
3 large eggs
$\frac{1}{2}$ tsp each nutmeg and cinnamon
Oil for deep-frying
Confectioners' sugar

PREPARATION:
1. Cook the raspberries with sugar to taste until soft, then sieve out all the seeds. Chill until required.

2. Blend the apricots with sufficient juice to give a smooth pouring sauce, then stir in the rum. Chill until required.

3. Sift the flour and salt onto a sheet of waxed paper.

4. Melt the butter with $\frac{3}{4}$ cup of water and bring to a rolling boil. Remove from the heat and pour in the flour and salt mixture all at once, then beat quickly to a stiff paste. Continue cooking and beating until the mixture comes clean away from the sides of the pan. Don't overbeat or the dough will become tough. Cool slightly.

5. Beat the eggs together, then gradually beat sufficient egg into the paste to produce a smooth and glossy batter. Add the nutmeg and cinnamon, mixing them well in. (The batter should be of a fairly soft, dropping consistency.)

6. When ready to cook, heat the oil in a deep-fryer to 350F. Drop small spoonfuls of batter carefully into the oil, and don't cook too many at a time. Cook for about 1 minute, removing the beignets when golden all over and drain on paper towels. Keep warm while you cook the rest.

7. Top the beignets with a little sieved confectioners' sugar before serving with both sauces, either warm or chilled.

LEMON TEQUILA SORBET (right)
This could almost be called a frozen cocktail and is unmistakeably alcoholic. More suitable for adults than kids!

Serves 4

INGREDIENTS:
3 lemons, scrubbed
Sprigs of lemon balm or lemon geranium, well washed
Scant cup sugar
5–6 tbsp tequila
1 egg white

PREPARATION:
1. Carefully remove the rind from two of the lemons,

avoiding the white pith. Place the rind with a sprig of herb and $1\frac{1}{2}$ cups of water in a pan with the sugar.

2. Gently bring the liquid to a boil, allowing the sugar time to dissolve. Boil rapidly for about 5 minutes until a light syrup forms.

3. Add the tequila, then strain into a freezer container. Add another sprig of herb, this time finely chopped. Cool, then freeze until ice crystals begin to form.

4. Whisk the egg white, then fold it into the partly-frozen sorbet. If you have an ice cream maker, transfer the mixture to this and process as recommended. Otherwise, return the mixture to the freezer container to firm up a little more.

5. Serve the sorbet when it is only just frozen, and add an extra touch of tequila if you wish.

Tip: Replace the lemon with lime or pink grapefruit mixed with lemon.

BAKED FRUITS WITH BOURBON CARAMEL GLAZE
Use the best available crisp, firm fruits, preferably when they are in season. Make the syrup with your preferred liqueur or dessert wine.

Serves 4

INGREDIENTS:
6 tbsp unsalted butter
6 tbsp light brown sugar
Juice and finely grated rind of 1 large orange
$1\frac{1}{2}$ lb fruit, for example, a mixture of ripe apples
 and pears, together with 12 oz sweet potato or squash
1 tsp vanilla extract
6 tbsp bourbon, liqueur or dessert wine
Freshly grated nutmeg

PREPARATION:
1. Melt the butter in a small roasting pan. Add the sugar and half the orange juice and rind and stir over gentle heat until the sugar has dissolved. Heat the oven to 350F.

2. Peel the fruit and sweet potato and cut them into neat slices or bite-sized cubes. Add them to the syrup immediately and stir to coat well. Then bake for about 40 minutes or until tender.

3. Transfer the pieces to a serving dish and keep warm if you wish. Pour the syrup into a small pan, add the rest of the orange juice and rind, the vanilla and the bourbon, liqueur or wine. Simmer gently for a few minutes until a syrupy consistency develops.

4. Serve warm or cool with the hot or cooled syrup and vanilla ice cream.

Tip: Store any leftover syrup in a jar in the fridge.

CREOLE ORANGES (above)
Refreshing but with a kick, these make a great dessert for any occasion, especially when served with Old-Fashioned Cookies (see opposite).

Serves 4

INGREDIENTS:
4 sweet oranges
1 cup sugar
2 tbsp water
4 tbsp rum or bourbon
A few sprigs of mint to garnish

PREPARATION:

1. Thinly remove the rind from 1 orange, using a potato peeler or sharp knife. Cut the rind into long julienne strips and place them in a small bowl of water.

2. Peel the rest of the oranges, avoiding the white pith, then divide the fruit into segments, cutting between the lines of the membranes and working over a bowl to catch the juice.

3. Place the sugar, orange juice and water in a small heavy-based pan and heat gently. When the sugar has completely dissolved, bring to a boil and continue to boil until the mixture begins to turn a pale caramel color. Remove from the heat and add the alcohol, stirring gently with a wooden spoon. Leave to partly cool.

4. Pour half the syrup over the oranges and set aside for several hours in a cold place to marinate. Leave the rest of the syrup to cool.

5. Serve the orange segments with the rest of the syrup spooned over, a few of the drained strips of orange rind, and a sprig of mint.

OLD-FASHIONED COOKIES

This is the kind of simple cookie so popular in the South. They could be flavored with coffee or spices, but these have the delicious aroma of vanilla.

Makes about 36

INGREDIENTS:
1 cup butter, softened
1 cup confectioners' sugar, sifted
1 large egg
$\frac{1}{2}$ tsp vanilla extract
$\frac{1}{2}$ tsp baking powder
$3\frac{1}{2}$ cups all-purpose flour, sifted
2–3 tbsp sugar

PREPARATION:

1. Cream the butter and confectioners' sugar together until smooth. Then gradually work in the egg, vanilla extract, baking powder and sufficient flour to give a very firm dough. (You can do this in a food processor if you prefer.)

2. Knead lightly until smooth, then wrap in plastic and chill for 30 minutes. Preheat the oven to 375F.

3. Divide the dough into 36 pieces and roll them into balls. Place the granulated sugar on a shallow plate and dip each ball into it, then place well apart (about 2 inches) on cookie sheets.

4. Using a clean dry rolling pin, flatten the dough balls slightly to form little circles. Bake for 12–15 minutes until they begin to turn golden, then leave them to cool on the sheets for 5 minutes. Transfer to a rack to cool completely.

5. Dust with more sifted confectioners' sugar before serving.

APPLE AND PECAN SUNDAES (left)

Make the caramel sauce in advance and store it in the refrigerator until required. It only takes a few minutes to reheat when needed, so you can enjoy the wicked toffee-apple flavor and the hot/cold contrast with ice cream at any time.

Serves 6

INGREDIENTS:
6 tbsp butter
1 large dessert apple, peeled, cored and sliced

¼ cup light brown sugar
¼ cup white sugar
Few drops of vanilla extract
¾ cup heavy cream or evaporated milk
12 scoops of vanilla or toffee ice cream
½ cup pecan nuts, chopped

PREPARATION:
1. Melt the butter in a heavy-based pan, add the apples, then cook for 2–3 minutes until just tender. Remove with a slotted spoon.

2. Add the sugars and vanilla extract to the pan and stir over a gentle heat until dissolved.

3. Pour in the cream or evaporated milk and cook for 3 minutes. Remove from the heat and set aside until required.

4. When ready to serve, place two scoops of ice cream into sundae glasses with the apples. Gently reheat the sauce, then spoon it over the ice cream, serving it immediately topped with the nuts.

DIVINE PECAN CAKE (left)
This is very, very rich! However, a little spice can be added which will help balance the sweetness.

Serves 10–12

INGREDIENTS:
Cake:
1½ cups pecan halves
3 cups all-purpose flour
1½ tsp baking powder
½ tsp salt
1 tbsp ground cinnamon
1 tbsp ground nutmeg
1 cup unsalted butter
1½ cups superfine sugar
5 eggs
1 tsp vanilla extract
2 tbsp milk

Frosting:
3 cups confectioners' sugar
3 egg whites, at room temperature
3–4 tbsp chocolate-nut spread

PREPARATION:
1. Set aside about 10 pecan halves for decoration. Meanwhile, place the remainder on an oven tray and roast at 350F for about 10 minutes, then whizz in a food processor, taking care not to chop the nuts too finely.

2. Grease, flour or line two or four 8-inch matching cake pans. Sift the dry ingredients together into a large bowl.

3. Cream the butter and sugar until pale and fluffy, then beat in the eggs, one at a time, adding a little flour to prevent separation. Blend in the rest of the flour mixture, the chopped nuts, vanilla, and sufficient milk to give a soft dropping consistency.

4. Divide the mixture evenly among the pans and bake for about 30 minutes if using two pans, 20–25 minutes if using four. When the cakes are just firm to the touch, leave to cool in the oven, then turn them out onto a tray or large board until completely cold.

5. Place the sifted confectioners' sugar and egg whites in a large mixing bowl over a pan of simmering water. Whisk, gradually increasing speed, until the mixture becomes thick, glossy and stands up in peaks.

6. If 2 pans have been used, cut the cakes to make 4 layers. Place the base layer on a board or serving plate, then stack up the others, covering the first and third layers with frosting, and using chocolate-nut spread on the middle layer. When all four layers are assembled, spread the sides and top with the rest of the white frosting and decorate with the reserved pecan halves.

Tip: If you have only two pans and need to split the cakes, be sure to chill them well before attempting to slice them horizontally.

PECAN PRALINES (overleaf left)
More a petit four than a cookie, you will see these delicious treats in street stalls wherever you go in the South. Make them as small as possible, and not too often, as they won't do your waistline any good!

Makes about 20

INGREDIENTS:
2 cups pecan halves
3 cups sugar (or a mix of granulated and light brown)

Pinch of salt
1 tsp vanilla extract
³/₄ cup evaporated milk
2 tbsp unsalted butter

PREPARATION:
1. Line 2 cookie sheets with non-stick or wax paper.
Set aside 10–20 pecan halves and chop the remainder,
but not too finely. Place them all on a flat tray to roast
at 350F for 10 minutes to draw out their unique aroma
and taste.

2. Place the sugar in a heavy-based pan with the salt,
vanilla and milk. Heat very gently until the sugar has
dissolved, then bring to a boil and stir in the warm
chopped nuts.

3. Allow the sugar to boil, then bubble gently, stirring
frequently until it reaches the soft ball stage (240F on a
sugar thermometer), or when a little syrup dropped
into ice-cold water forms a soft ball.

4. Remove from the heat, then beat hard for a minute.
Drop teaspoons of the mixture onto the cookie sheets
and top each one with a half or piece of pecan nut.
Leave until cold, then store in an airtight container.

CREOLE RICE CALAS (Fried Rice Cakes) (above)
*These should always be considered when there is leftover
rice and you don't know what to do with it. Calas are
fried balls of rice and dough that are eaten covered
with powdered sugar, and are not unlike rice-filled
beignets. It was told to me that long ago, on cold
mornings in New Orleans, the cry of 'CALAS! CALAS!
TOUTES CHAUDES!' could be heard coming from the
French Quarter, where Creole women made and sold
these special delicacies.*

INGREDIENTS:
6 tbsp all-purpose flour
3 heaped tbsp sugar
2 tsp baking powder
¼ tsp salt
2 cups cooked rice
2 eggs
¼ tsp vanilla extract
Pinch of nutmeg
Oil for frying
Confectioners' sugar

PREPARATION:
1. Mix together the flour, sugar, baking powder and salt. Thoroughly mix the rice, eggs and vanilla extract together in a separate bowl. Add the dry ingredients to the rice and egg mixture.

2. When thoroughly mixed, drop spoonfuls into hot fat in a deep-fryer heated to about 350F and cook until brown. Drain on paper towels.

3. Sprinkle with confectioners' sugar and serve while hot. Another way of serving them is coated with honey or cane syrup instead of sugar.

MISSISSIPPI MUD PIE (below)
Also called Black Bottom Pie because of the rich, dark chocolate base and wickedly sticky filling.

Serves 8

INGREDIENTS:
Pie shell:
1 oz cocoa powder
3 oz butter or margarine

cookies. Press the mixture evenly into the base and up the sides of a 9-inch fluted cake pan. Preheat the oven to 375F.

2. For the filling, cream together the butter and sugar, gradually beat in the eggs with the cocoa powder, then stir in the melted chocolate, followed by the cream and vanilla extract.

3. Spoon the filling into the pie shell and bake for about 35 minutes until almost set. Reduce the oven temperature to 325F.

4. Whisk the egg whites until stiff, then gradually whisk in the sugar until the mixture is thick and glossy and holds in peaks. Spoon onto the warm filling, using a spoon to make peaks on the surface, and return to the oven for 10–15 minutes, or until the meringue is cooked but not too brown.

5. Allow to cool and serve warm or cold with confectioners' sugar sifted over.

PLUM OAT CRISP (left)

Use fresh red, black or yellow plums when they are available. If you cannot find fresh ones, use canned plums instead.

Serves 4

INGREDIENTS:
12 oz fresh plums or the equivalent canned
Sugar to taste
Juice of $\frac{1}{2}$ orange
1 cup all-purpose flour
4 tbsp butter or margarine
$\frac{2}{3}$ cup porridge oats
3–4 tbsp fresh breadcrumbs
2 tbsp dark brown sugar, or to taste

PREPARATION:
1. Cut the fresh plums in half, remove the pits, and cook briefly with a little sugar and the orange juice until they begin to soften. If using canned plums, don't cook them at all, but add the orange juice, with sugar only if necessary.

2. Rub the flour and butter together to form a fine crumbly texture. Add the oats, crumbs and brown sugar and mix well. Preheat the oven to 375F.

3. Place the fruit in an ovenproof dish and sprinkle on the topping. Bake for 30 minutes until the topping is

3 tbsp maple syrup
8 oz crushed crumbs made from graham crackers or gingersnaps

Filling:
$\frac{3}{4}$ cup butter
$1\frac{1}{2}$ cups dark brown sugar
4 large eggs
4 tbsp cocoa powder
5 oz plain chocolate, melted
$1\frac{1}{4}$ cups light cream
1 tsp vanilla extract

Meringue:
2 large egg whites
1 cup confectioners' sugar
Sifted confectioners' sugar

PREPARATION:
1. To make the pie shell, melt the cocoa, butter and syrup together and blend well, then add the crushed

golden and serve with heavy cream, English custard or ice cream.

PECAN PIE (below)

This is an irresistible New Orleans classic, originating from the early days of pecan growing in Louisiana. Serve with whipped cream or vanilla ice cream.

Serves 8

INGREDIENTS:
9-inch pre-baked pie shell (can be bought)
$1/2$ cup superfine sugar
Scant cup light brown sugar
$3/4$ cup butter, melted
4 very large eggs
1 tsp vanilla extract
$2/3$ cup pecan nuts, chopped
1 cup pecan halves
Superfine sugar for sprinkling

PREPARATION:

1. Place the pie shell on a cookie sheet. Preheat the oven to 400F.

2. Melt the two sugars and the butter slowly in a pan until the sugar dissolves. Cool slightly. Beat the eggs in a large bowl, then beat in the sugar-butter mixture and the vanilla extract.

3. Stir in the chopped nuts and pour carefully into the pie shell. Bake for 15–20 minutes, then arrange the halved nuts neatly on the top. Bake for a further 20 minutes or until the filling is firm to the touch.

BAKED BANANAS FOSTER (above)

Now world-famous, this simple dish was created at Brennan's Restaurant in the French Quarter of New Orleans and is served there to this day. Oranges are not always added, but they do complement the sweet richness of the dish.

Serves 3–4

INGREDIENTS:
4 tbsp unsalted butter
Scant $1/2$ cup sugar
4 bananas, peeled and cut in half lengthways
3 tbsp banana liqueur
2 oranges, peeled and segmented avoiding pith

75

1 vanilla pod, split down its length and cut into 4
4 tbsp rum
Vanilla ice cream

PREPARATION:
1. Melt the butter and sugar in a small pan and stir until the sugar has dissolved, then add the bananas and liqueur. Preheat the oven to 350F.

2. Take 4 sheets of aluminum foil, sufficient to make individual parcels, and place them on cookie sheets. Divide the bananas evenly between the sheets, adding a few orange segments.

3. Spoon the sauce over the bananas, adding a piece of vanilla to each parcel. Fold up the foil to make sealed parcels and bake in the oven until the bananas soften and turn brown (about 15 minutes).

4. Place each parcel on a heatproof plate, tipping some of the juices into a small pan. Add the rum to the pan and ignite it, then spoon it over the bananas while it is still flaming.

5. Serve immediately with ice cream.

NEW ORLEANS-STYLE PAIN PERDU (right)
The French influence still permeates Creole cooking, clearly evident in some of its most economical dishes. This lovely version of French toast, or "lost bread," is delicious served with baked fruits or vanilla ice cream.

Serves 2

INGREDIENTS:
2 slices of slightly stale white bread, crusts removed
1 medium egg, beaten
1–2 tbsp whisky or rum
4 tbsp unsalted butter
1 tbsp superfine sugar
Freshly grated nutmeg

PREPARATION:
1. Cut the slices of bread into neat quarters, then beat the egg, 1 tablespoon of water and the whisky together in a shallow dish. Dip the slices in this and turn them over until all the egg is absorbed into the bread.

2. Heat the butter in a pan until it bubbles, then add

the bread. Turn it over as soon as it turns golden underneath and cook on the second side for ¹⁄₂–1 minute.

3. Transfer to heated serving plates, sprinkling immediately with the sugar and nutmeg.

BANANA BREAD-AND-BUTTER PUDDING (right)
Bread-and-butter pudding is delicious enough as it is, but the addition of bananas makes it even more sumptuous.

Serves 4

INGREDIENTS:
6 slices of stale white bread, lightly buttered
Brown sugar
2 large bananas, sliced
2 oz currants or raisins
3 eggs
1¹⁄₄ cups whole milk
1 tbsp superfine sugar

PREPARATION:

1. Sprinkle the buttered bread with a little brown sugar. Cut the slices into quarters or halves.

2. Arrange the bread, buttered side down, in an ovenproof dish, layering it with the bananas and half the currants or raisins.

3. Mix the eggs, milk and sugar together and pour over the bread, leaving for 10–15 minutes so that the mixture is fully absorbed. Preheat the oven to 350F.

4. When the bread has soaked up all the liquid, sprinkle the rest of the fruit on top and bake for about 30 minutes.

5. Sprinkle the top with a little more brown sugar before serving with a rum or whisky custard or cream.

BROWNIES WITH PECAN TOFFEE SAUCE (overleaf)
Brownies are a wonderful dessert, especially when served with toffee-nut sauce and vanilla ice cream.

Makes 16 squares

INGREDIENTS:
Brownies:
$3/4$ cup butter or margarine
Scant cup dark brown sugar
2 eggs, beaten

1–2 tbsp light corn syrup, warmed
1 oz cocoa powder, sifted
$\frac{1}{2}$ cup whole-grain flour
2 tsp ground ginger

Pecan Toffee Sauce:
1 cup pecan halves, lightly toasted or roasted
1 cup dark corn syrup
$\frac{1}{2}$ cup unsalted butter
3 oz dark chocolate, broken into pieces

PREPARATION:
1. Preheat the oven to 350F. Grease and line a deep 7-inch square cake pan.

2. Cream together the butter and sugar until fluffy. Add the eggs, syrup and dry ingredients, blending them together until smooth.

3. Spoon the mixture into the pan and level the top. Bake for 35–40 minutes or until firm. Leave in the pan to cool slightly.

4. Put the ingredients for the sauce into a heavy-based saucepan, gently stirring them together until well blended. Bring to a boil, still stirring.

5. To serve, cut the warm brownies into squares, top with ice cream, and pour on the pecan sauce.

TRIPLE CHOCOLATE MUFFINS (left)
Light and fluffy, these may be highly caloric but they are delicious at any time of the day, preferably eaten warm. Make up a batch and freeze some ready to reheat when you have a sudden invasion of kids in your home.

Makes 6–8 large muffins

INGREDIENTS:
3 cups all-purpose flour, sieved
3 tsp baking powder
2 oz cocoa powder, sieved
$\frac{1}{3}$ cup dark brown sugar
2 oz dark bitter chocolate, broken into pieces
2 tbsp melted butter
1 large egg
Scant cup milk, warmed
1 oz each white and dark chocolate chips

PREPARATION:
1. Preheat the oven to 350F. Mix the dry ingredients together.

2. Melt the chocolate and half the butter together with a little milk until blended. Beat the egg and the remaining milk and butter together. Stir into the dry ingredients along with the chocolate, and combine lightly to produce a soft mixture.

3. Lightly stir in the chocolate chips. Spoon into muffin cups and bake for 20–25 minutes until the muffins are well risen and just firm. Serve at once or reheat slightly just before serving.

Variations:
1. Chocolate Orange Muffins: leave out the block chocolate and add another 4 tablespoons of sugar. Instead of the milk, substitute the juice and finely grated rind of 2 large oranges plus sufficient milk to give 1 cup of liquid.

2. Chocolate and Pecan Muffins: replace the cocoa powder with sieved flour and use light brown sugar instead of dark. Add several drops of vanilla extract to the basic dough and at the last minute stir in 2 oz each toasted pecan nuts and chopped milk chocolate instead of the white and dark chocolate chips.